Contents

III. Patterns of Thought

IV. Beyond the Rules

A Dirty Little Book About Writing the Truth

Creative Essay Writing Beyond Formulas

Rich Ives

Owl Creek Press
1620 N. 45th St.
Seattle WA 98103

Acknowledgments

Special thanks to the students in my writing classes for helping to develop and test the ideas contained in this book, and to my fellow teachers and writers whose examples have helped to make both teaching and writing much more than academic experiences. Without their patience, encouragement and enthusiasm, this book would not have been possible. May you all be so fortunate with your fellow travelers.

A Dirty Little Book About
Writing the Truth

V. The Writing Life

Introduction

This book is a combination of approaches designed to provide a practical yet creative view of essay writing as a skill with unlimited applications. Part I provides a framework within which writers may view and discuss typical problems and questions common to all writing. Part II uses five major elements of writing to discuss the relationship of essay writing to other writing forms, particularly fiction, drama and poetry, and to suggest how these elements of writing are linked and can be developed in relation to each other. Part III introduces some common essay organization strategies through discussion of thought patterns and offers suggestions for discovering and advancing them. These patterns are presented in a cumulative sequence that allows each new method the benefits of the writer's growing knowledge and experience with previous methods to contribute to efforts towards mastering the new method. Part IV provides possibilities for exploring beyond the more basic concepts of the first three parts and Part V returns to the idea of writing as an element of daily life to discuss the realities of a writer's world.

All explanatory materials are focused on clarifying possibilities and approaches, not prescribing them. The emphasis is on doing this without oversimplifying any more than is necessary for clarity. This book is not a prescription for doing it "right" but a framework to encourage discovery. This is a book about the potential that writers will find in creative application of common patterns and techniques. To explain too much by providing an outline of the "proper" way to do it would not help writers develop the kinds of problem solving abilities and constructive attitudes that lead to growth. Frequent reminders are present that exceptions not only exist but are desirable and stimulating. Most of the jungle's rules can be broken, but it's a good idea to understand the inhabitants first.

Writing is a processing of experience in the same way that life is. Writing can recreate that experience with a more focused clarity about its meaning. It gains understanding by risking simplification. When a balance between reliving the experience and the writer's interpretation of its essence is achieved, it both distills and sets in motion once more the experience that initiated it, allowing the reader to experience and understand it as the writer has, but this time without the delay of the writer's sorting and focusing of its meaning. And writing can do this with experience the writer has not even literally had. Even in nonfiction, imagination can provide other types of experience and understanding as essential to our "reality" as anything we might think of as "fact." This allows us to live in a larger universe and expand not only our understanding of life but our involvement in it.

I am a teacher as well as a writer because I often learn new paths to the treasure from watching those I am guiding test the possibilities as well as follow the trail. If both experiences are present, I can teach as I wish to live, as a willing and excitable student of life. Writing can and should be participation in life at the deepest possible levels of awareness and growth. Writing is not merely a tool, it's the visible result of knowledge and experience as it is processed by a unique and fully engaged human being. Writing is its own reason, as life is.

And, as in life, truth in writing exists on many levels. Only the most simple among us is satisfied with oversimplification and the deceptions of mere facts. You have to learn to walk, but it doesn't explain where to go when you can. Progress in writing is not merely a matter of learning rules, though guidelines can help if approached with an appreciation for exceptions and differences. Good writing is a search for the universal through the uniqueness of the individual. It does not abandon the individual for the crowd.

I. The World in the Words

The Perpetual Student

All writers remain students if they continue to develop their craft. This continual development is an essential element behind the best writing of professionals. Good writers benefit from an ambitious attitude. It is better to attempt much and partially fail than to attempt little and achieve it. Writers participate in an ongoing dialogue of ideas and techniques with other writers as well as with readers. They become active participants in the world's history of ideas and understanding. Writing is thinking in words, and human thinking, as well as human language, is constantly progressing. Our best writers don't just attempt to keep up with this change. They encourage and coax and sometimes lead its progress. "Expert" is not a very useful word among writers because writing is not simply a body of knowledge to be mastered but a complex relationship of possibilities and choices. Good writing is not "perfect," merely an effective balance of its elements, and new ways of effectively balancing elements are constantly emerging. Good writers do not continue to rely on the same "tricks" of their trade that have worked in the past, though they certainly use them to build on. Progress in writing, then, is often relative, first of all to the writer's previous work and, ultimately, to the body of existing writing available to the reader.

The processes of discovery and learning about writing that a beginning writer must immerse in, as open-mindedly as possible, are essentially the same as the ones a professional writer begins anew with each new essay. There is no reason for a beginning writer to feel the task at hand is going to produce "amateur" results. While experience and guided practice will improve the odds of greater success, the opportunity to create an effective and original piece of writing is available to every writer willing to fully explore the possibilities of each new subject with an eye towards applying new skills and ideas and an eager and involved attitude towards making discoveries. A writer's fascination with his subject is an opportunity to share the basic joys of childhood again. Even the most complex scientific or philosophical ideas benefit in writing from the enthusiasm of the writer, the childlike wonder of discovery, of new life.

Involve yourself with your subject and measure your success by the increasing effectiveness of your writing on readers and by the renewed excitement you feel discovering more about what you can do. Strive not to be perfect but to be better each time you write. Let your writing delight you. Once engaged in your experience in this way, you will have a far greater reason to learn.

Subject

When learning to write, it's a good idea to give yourself the advantage of writing about something you're curious about. It's often suggested that you should write about what you know, but don't stop with what you know. Write to discover as well as to inform. Don't let yourself drift into a subtle suggestion of superiority by writing only what makes you superior to your readers because you know it better. Explore your subject, don't just explain it. Let the reader watch over your shoulder as you learn as well as inform. Desire for the adventure of gaining knowledge often provides an underlying support for good writing. Write not only what you know, but what you want to know. Good writing nearly always contains an exploration of the unknown, even when the starting point is something known thoroughly. The act of using language is an adventure. Enjoy it.

Help yourself in this process by asking questions about your relationship to your subject. Why are you writing about *this* subject? What is your attitude towards it, your personal focus? What has caused you to feel this way? Often, there is a second or hidden subject in the writing. Search for it, and draw it out as you develop your work.

When you become more aware of the hidden subjects in your work, you will find it easier to develop interest in a broader range of subjects. This process of questioning and digging becomes a source of support for the value of anything you write. It helps reveal what really matters to you. This is so essential to good writing because style reveals many things about the author's attitude towards the subject. If it doesn't really matter to you, it will show. This is also the main source of errors in grammar and sentence structure. These problems are more likely to occur if there is a conflict of interest going on. If you're writing something that isn't captivating your whole attention, you are more likely to do it awkwardly and confuse the reader.

Discovery

A writer writing is like a man building a chicken coop in a high wind. He grabs onto any board he can and nails it down fast.
—William Faulkner

Trust the man who seeks the truth.
Beware the one who has found it.
—anonymous

I didn't mean to say it, but I meant what I said.
—James McMurtry

Nurture a fresh sense of attention. Notice things. Revel in detail. A good writer is often someone who can become deeply engulfed in things other people would not notice. A good writer hungers for a more complete experience and it can be a more complete experience of a snail or a drop of water or the pattern the clouds make as you daydream on the grass as easily as a great idea or a profound understanding of a complex relationship.

Don't just write essays. Build them. Put them together like a scrapbook and then shape them like a sculpture. Donald Murray says, "Craft is what you do; art is what somebody else says you have done, usually after you're dead." Craft is used to build things. Build your essay with enough thought, care, and depth, and it may become art. Build it in stages. Don't just write it, develop it. A good writer is willing to encourage even the most tentative possibilities and attempt to push what is being written out to the edges of what it can be. This almost never happens on the first draft, though the first draft nearly always contains the seeds of several potentially great essays. The good writer is learning to sift through the ordinary dirt and chaff for the seed which is ready to sprout. This sifting and sorting must occur before the essay can take root.

Don't hold anything back when you're starting. Kick the "critic" part of your brain out of the room when writing first drafts. Trust your impulses no matter how surprising or apparently unrelated they may seem. Concentrate on enjoying the freedom to wander and search. Don't get tied up in, "What's the right way?" Just do it *your* way, the way the impulse strikes you at this moment. There are no wrong ways on the first draft. You shouldn't be expecting to use all that you write at this stage. Just set things in motion and begin digging for the gems. Calvin Trillin calls the first draft "the vomit all."

Later on, the "critic" function can enter and help you shape this raw material, but if the writer can't use the freedom and adventure of enjoyable exploration to establish an engaging relationship to a subject, there will be little of real interest to shape. It's much easier to edit out the excess than to effectively insert the missing, though both will be needed. First drafts usually work best when they lean towards too much rather than too little. Use them to wander and speculate. Where might this go if I let it?

To write well is to learn about yourself as well as to provide information to others. Writing well is an act of discovery, just as reading is. It is also learning to think and to notice, to become more aware. Good writers are continually becoming more complete, sensitive and thoughtful human beings. They may pose radical opinions or champion causes they don't completely believe in just to awaken their thoughts and sensitivities and to question their opinions. A good writer is a speculator, someone who pursues possibilities rather than merely reports existing knowledge. A good writer expands our awareness even when our opinions have not been changed. A good writer is willing to risk being wrong simply to discover the meaning of a viewpoint. A good writer is a relentless hunter, even when the existence of the prey is uncertain. Good writers trust in the possibilities of the results of the hunt because they are fascinated with the process. Their journey is as valuable as their destination. Sometimes they reach new conclusions, sometimes they reaffirm previous conclusions with greater understanding. Good writers, like good readers, are perpetual students; they learn from what they do, and what they do is continually encounter the new. Only pushing on the edges of what we know can keep us in the world of the new. Such questioning is essential to the development of good writing and good writers.

In early writing courses, students are usually taught the thesis sentence and encouraged to carefully organize their information. What students should be learning from this is clear thinking, not rules. Clear thinking may involve simplifying, but it does not have to be presented to the reader as boredom. By the time students have reached the stage of clear thinking in developing any piece of writing, they may also be in grave danger of writing only what they have already decided they think. What they may be about to write becomes an afterthought. The discovery that good writing provides occurs in and during the writing (and, therefore, during the reading). It is a shared discovery, a journey with the reader, who questions the writer's choices as the journey continues. These questions may be stated or merely responded to, but an awareness that this experience is really a dialogue shows in the structure and direction good writing pursues. When this does not happen, the result is very similar to that incredibly boring conversation we've all had with the person who begins with a question only to proceed to politely show us that he or she already has the only solution. This kind of person, and writer, was never really interested in our involvement in the discussion.

Getting Started

Sooner or later, all writers find that they are either "blocked" or in a rut. When this happens, it's time to think about our attitudes and approaches to writing. Most likely, it's what we bring to the writing before we even start that creates this and we should try to identify what it is that's limiting us. We can do this by thinking about the process or by getting started in a new and unfamiliar way. Here are a few possibilities to help shake up limiting attitudes.

1. The most common difficulty for essay writers experiencing writer's block is a preconception of what the writing is supposed to be. This can be at war with the writer's own more personal desire for the freedom to make this new adventure his own. Most of these preconceptions are false limits on what the essay can be and when they are named, this becomes more apparent. Try writing a list of what an essay is. If you find your list dry and boring, maybe you should think of what you're going to do as something other than an essay until your concept of an essay has changed.

Often, in an overzealous attempt to get our writing organized, we are taught limits that clarify the most basic of writing elements in ways we receive as prescriptions for correctness. Good writing is not "correct." Good writing is searching, and only when we are thoroughly lost do we need such limits. Don't get so busy looking at the compass that you don't notice the beauty of the moss on the trees. Experience where you are in your writing with pleasure and observation before you worry about whether or not it's the right place.

One cross-disciplinary idea that has served many artists well is that artistic achievement is a matter of taking what you're doing far enough. This applies even if what you are doing is, by existing standards, "wrong." A bad idea can become interesting, even turn into a good idea, if it's taken far enough. If you notice something in your writing that appears weak or incorrect, don't forget that you can choose to strengthen it with further emphasis or deliberate repetition as well as eliminate it. Many artistic discoveries have come from pursuing a "wrong" way to do it far enough. A good writer wants to explore the possibilities of the wilderness as well as find the path.

Beginning your work with an attitude of freedom and excitement will go a long way towards eliminating "writer's block." Even if you are writing for an assignment, you are not doing this for someone else, not really. This is yours and the assignment is merely specifying which edge of the wilderness you will start on.

2. Keep a notebook. Write in it impulsively, not worrying about what it will be used for or whether or not it might make an essay. Use it to reinforce the connection between your ordinary daily life and words. Put things in it you would not expect to find in a journal. Let the unexpected coincidences of impulses in different moods create unexpected neighbors in your notebook. After you've done this for a while, you will probably find surprising repeated ideas and obsessions that you didn't realize you were so frequently entertaining. To a writer, obsession is often a friend. We all have themes that haunt us and the good writers keep returning to them and developing them.

3. Try thinking of your writing as directed at a very specific audience, preferably a single person, and address him or her as if you were talking or writing a letter. You may find useful effects from the way in which you will adjust your way of saying it to this person you are addressing. This person need not be named or revealed for the effects to be useful, though sometimes it is helpful to do so.

4. Write about your experience of frustration, anxiety or confusion at the difficulty you are experiencing with your writing. Not only may you be limited by unnecessary preconceptions of what an essay is supposed to be, you may also be limited by the screen of another subject blocking the way. Write about what you are most immediately experiencing to make room for the next experience.

5. Try speaking your essay into a tape recorder, rather than writing it, for your first draft. You will not only say different things, you will also say them in different ways. For most of us, the way we have been taught to write and the choices we have made about our reading have created a "written" voice which is not the same as our "speaking" voice. The rhythms and effects of each are different and we can benefit from using both of them.

6. Try *telling* someone *about* your essay and recording what you say. Then let them ask you questions and answer them without any limits. Do not show them your writing. You may discover this way that something important or better said was not contained as well in your writing as it was in your spoken responses. This can provide a more immediate awareness of the curiosities and likely reactions of your audience, which can then be worked into the organization of your written essay. This approach may create a different angle of view towards your writing that could provide useful perspective and new ways of saying.

7. Write when you don't have anything to say. Get over the idea that you have to be "inspired" to write well. You may start with writing that you won't like, but writing seldom stays in one place. If you can get started, it will go somewhere. All you have to do is keep the words flowing. This will be hardest for those

with the most preconceived ideas of an essay's "limits."

8. Most of us carry a sense of place with us into our writing. Try deliberately changing the location the writing is coming from. Imagine you are in a different country, a different home, a different state of mind, a different season, a different world, and see how this affects the way in which you present your voice.

9. Try concentrating on two or more specific technical elements, such as short sentences and large words, or an unusual way of speaking and an ordinary subject or theme. One element is usually too limiting to create enough that is new and unexpected. Try elements you feel a little uncomfortable with, to expand your range. Get engrossed in the possibilities of the way your selected elements can be used. Let them take you over. Let them have their way with you. Forget about subjects or goals. Just let the uniqueness of unexpected utterances carry you away. Then pause and look back over what you have written for theme and idea. Now add contrast and continue working in your more usual modes. Consider returning to the experiment whenever you feel routine setting in.

10. Write a story and an essay and then turn the story into an essay and the essay into a story. You may discover that being focused on a different form when writing the first draft helps keep the second draft fresh as you "translate" it into the new form. You will probably try not to lose the qualities of the first draft form as you shape it into the new form and the combination can revitalize your work. Try this with a poem and an essay. Try it with a short play, a letter, a memo, etc.

11. Go for a walk. Exercise. This can encourage you to think about the work before writing it. For me, it also

creates a little taboo that I love breaking. I'm supposed to be exercising, not writing. So I think about writing the whole time I'm exercising and by the time I'm done exercising, the writing is ready to pour out. The health nuts will tell you there's a physical reaction to the exercise and go into great detail about endorphins and biochemical reactions, but maybe it's just having your mind free because your body's preoccupied. Or maybe it's just finding something else you're supposed to be doing that's good for you so writing can be fun instead of demanding. Good writing is about the desire to participate and experience more fully. It's not your hidden parental voice saying, "Take your vitamins. They're good for you."

12. Think visually. Start with a picture instead of words. Let an image lead you into what you have to say. If one doesn't easily offer itself from your own ideas and experiences, use a book or magazine. It's not the starting point that matters here. It's the reaction. Follow it and nudge it along when it falters. Don't worry about where it's going. Worry about keeping it moving. Keep reacting. Try this with each of the other senses as well.

13. Start in the middle. Another common reason for writer's block is wanting the opening to be great. You can't go on until you come up with the right beginning. So don't start at the beginning. Enjoy the excitement of ideas already in motion. Force this by starting or stopping mid-sentence if you must. Try using fragments. Write a paragraph or two and then write what came before, not after. Change your expectations of order. Live your writing out of order and see what you feel, what you learn. Understanding often does not arrive chronologically.

14. Use contrast. Whatever you've been doing, try doing the opposite. Not because what you've been doing is wrong, but because it can be made clearer, more dramatic, more effective by being placed next to its opposite. Good writing is about conflict because life is full of conflict. And conflict can be created and clarified by contrast.

15. Read. Read. Read. When you can't write, read. Sometimes it just takes getting reacquainted with words and the patterns they create. Writers don't read to copy other writers, though they may learn a great deal from them. They read to renew the excitement and energy of participating in the dialogue of reader and writer. Reading establishes a communication and breaks your struggle with a solo existence. When a dialogue's there, inertia has been at least partially broken. When this dialogue of reader and writer exists, you only have to switch sides, not start something completely new. You will have established a relationship to words common to both sides of the dialogue.

16. Try not to think about anything. Serious meditators may disagree, but for most of us who have not trained to do it, this is impossible. But it will help eliminate the static, the unimportant, the unnecessary. Many writers write in locations so familiar that their surroundings are boring. This encourages their imagination. Perhaps the conscious mind goes to sleep and the subconscious takes over. What surfaces may well be the deeper, more important subject that was just waiting for the daily garbage to get taken care of. Good writers learn to pay attention to their subconscious.

17. Include your dreams in your notebook and write them down as soon as you can after having them. They may seem chaotic and senseless, but over time, patterns will emerge, and you may well find these patterns

emerging in writing which is not about dreams as well. The relationship between the conscious and the subconscious life is an underlying subject for most good writers. Nurture the relationship between your dreams and your daily reality by writing about both.

18. Listen to the way others speak. If you read much, you're already doing this with the written voice, but pay the same kind of attention to the spoken voice. There are many occasions in writing, the use of quotes in characterization being only the most obvious, which benefit from the sense of a speaking, rather than a written, voice. Pay attention to the variety of spoken voices available to you. Try speaking in someone else's voice, on paper.

19. "Get off the subject." This advice is from Richard Hugo, the poet and teacher, and it is meant for poets, but there is no reason an essay can't have the same surprise and pleasure in the unexpected as a poem often does. This works because it's not likely you will really succeed. You may say something which appears to be unrelated and find as you continue that it is, after all, related, but in a less obvious way. Do this when you feel your essay is getting boring, expected, too obvious. Many writers fear that they will not make sense, when it is often making too much "sense" which has created the weakness. It can turn their writing into a predictable and uninteresting rehash of the same old idea repeated over and over again to be sure the reader "got it."

The Government of Tongues; Grammar, Rules, and Effective Communication

Yes, words long faded may again revive
and words may fade now blooming and alive.
If usage wills it so, to whom belongs
the rule and law? The government of tongues.

—Horace

There isn't a rule in writing that can't be successfully broken. No, I'm not absolutely sure this is true, but I've been challenging my classes with this statement for more than ten years now and so far, we haven't found one that doesn't have an exception.

"Rules" in writing are not laws. They are guidelines for clear communication and they change as our needs for communication change. This is why it is far more important to question rules and gain an understanding of why they usually help us communicate effectively than it is to memorize them. If writing were essentially a matter of learning rules, machines would be able to do it for us much better than they can. Machines can't work without rules. But people work with the assistance of rules as guidelines to help them perform more complex tasks than machines are capable of. The rules exist to help us use our language. When they no longer do this well, they change. Our language is flexible enough to allow us to perform incredibly complicated tasks, and the tasks we ask of it change over time. The "rules" must reflect these changes. The people who use the language are the ultimate rule makers.

While certain kinds of "understandings" are helpful to clear communication, it is a backwards approach to learn the rules first without focusing on their reasons for being. Numerous grammar errors are a result of muddled thinking, not ignorance of rules.

26

Concentrate on clear communication first. What makes your meaning clear to the reader? If you can remain focused on this, you will make fewer "mistakes."

Since the most important purpose of language is clarity and the reader is your yardstick of success, don't forget your common sense about dealing with people. You are not only trying to be clear, you are also trying to gain your reader's trust to assist you with that clarity. Treat your readers as equals to avoid losing them with a superior attitude. Imagine yourself as the reader as well as the writer. You won't talk down to yourself unless you have a very serious self-esteem problem.

And if you have been learning to read with greater involvement, like a writer looking for tricks and possibilities, like a reader who wants all of the information contained in how it's written as well as what it's written about, you will be paying a kind of attention when you read that will help you spot problems when you write. You will begin to spot trouble because it looks wrong, because it feels awkward. You will be gathering a more subliminal sense of rhythms and logic and structure.

And don't forget what engages and what bores you as a reader. Writing to "rules" tends to create repetition when your reader wants variety, especially in your sentence structures, which represent your thought patterns. The reader wants to experience the delight of surprise in your ideas and manner of presentation. Just like you do when you're the reader. Writing is a dialogue. Keep it lively.

Becoming a good writer is a constant process of questioning and trying out possible solutions. This is no less true for the professional writer than for the beginning student. While it is certainly important to learn how most people use the language, in order to know what is expected, many writing courses get so involved in perfecting "proper" usage that they encourage the writer to give only what is "expected" and lose sight of the wonderful varieties and possibilities of effective surprise. The real difference between life and writing is that surprise in writing may have occurred in a rough draft, without forethought, as it sometimes does in life, but a choice must then be made to keep it and even enhance its effect. In choosing not to change it, it becomes deliberate. If the reader then experiences it as a surprise, he will do so by the writer's choice, even when that choice first became possible by accident.

It's incredibly difficult to know what doing things differently means if you don't know you're doing things differently. But it is equally dangerous to effective writing to always labor primarily to be "correct." "Correct" writing may get approval and never be read outside the classroom because it simply isn't very interesting. "Correct" writers are often not good communicators, only reliable followers of rules.

And so goes the struggle to make writing interesting and effective. And from the struggle comes discovery. Good writing includes the struggle as well as the discovery. Good writing involves the reader, just as it involved the writer, in actively making the discovery. Good writing asks for involvement. It takes risks willingly because that is how discoveries are made. Good writers then shape the reader's involvement, but offer more than just conclusions. They let us share in the process of discovery that the writing represents.

Questioning Authority

Education may be in even more danger than it always has been when job-oriented learning dominates to the point of creating learning models which are little more than memorization routines. This may seem an odd place to bring up such a notion, but in language use we are dealing with information exchange that occurs in many ways we will not even begin to realize if we presume good writing is a matter of learning to "do it the right way." One of the more common perceptions of "the right way" is the "business world" way. But even in the business world, there is mass boredom and very ineffective communication when a single "right way" gets too dominant.

Good writing is fresh, alive with new possibilities, and the new is never created by being simply "right." A thoughtfully presented question is often more interesting than a "right" answer. Being "right" is not always desirable for a writer. Being interesting is.

The desire to question is a character trait well worth cultivating. Enthusiasm and curiosity encourage and shape good writing as well as active lives. They help a writer maintain active involvement in the subject. No reader wants to work harder to stay involved in the writing than the writer did, but most will invest a great deal of thought in a piece of writing that rewards their efforts to question and learn.

Nonfiction: What Is Truth?

It may be helpful to an essay writer to try to place what he or she is attempting to do into a context, and we may tend to do this naturally, intuitively, without even carefully thinking about it. The writer may, for example, presume the basic difference between an essay and a story is that the essay is true and the story is made up. But doesn't any good story contain a truth? And what if the essay happens to be about a "theory" or an "opinion?" Is it no longer "the truth?" And what, then, is "autobiographical fiction" or "creative nonfiction?"

It is likely that beginning writers may tend to restrict what they do in an essay. There are certain restrictions when writing an essay for a specific context, such as a history paper, but even here the writer's conceptions of expectations may be unnecessarily limiting and the writer should be questioning them. Questioning is the nature of good writing.

One of the great discoveries of contemporary writing has been the recognition that virtually all of the possibilities of fiction and poetry are available, in one way or another, to essay writing, and many of our best fiction writers and poets write fascinating essays. Conveying useful information does not have to be boring, and by learning more about the possibilities of new approaches, the essay writer can actually convey more information with fewer words, traditionally the job of the poet.

This is not to say that an essay writer has the freedom to lie, but an essay writer does have the freedom (and responsibility) to speculate and to try out possibilities, even to create imaginary "stories" to demonstrate a point (the example method).

And now we have come to a more important distinction between an essay and a story or poem. When asked about the "message" of one of his poems, Robert

Frost is reported to have said, "I send my messages by Western Union." A great work of fiction or poetry resists summation. It is already a carefully considered condensation of life. A good essay is also a condensation, but it does have a point, and a thoughtful reader should be certain it is there, even if it may not be easily expressed. It may be useful to the essay writer to provide all the information necessary to understand the point without actually summing it up; nevertheless, the point must be there. The point may arise from a situation or consideration of possibilities rather than exist before the essay is written. The point may even change, for the author receptive to new discoveries, during the course of the writing, but it needs to be there because the reader needs to understand why this information was gathered. The reader does not ask this of a story or a poem. It is the job of the story or poem to be "alive" and if in the process of living, a point is made, this is an unexpected bonus. But it is the job of an essay to present information organized for some apparent (at least by the end of the essay) reason, a point. The meaning of this point must be supported with detail, in other words, "earned." An essay can also, like fiction or poetry, be "alive," but the reader will ask why and expect an answer.

Audience

As an author, you have the potential for reaching millions of people with your writing, but you must do this in millions of one-on-one exchanges. It's helpful to a writer to view the audience not as a large mass of "average" readers, but as individuals. Reading is a dialogue with the writer. Only two people can participate at a time. Even when an author reads his or her own work publicly, there is often a sense of personal connection created by the intimacy of revelations the author is shaping, by suggestion and implication as well as statement. Readers are being asked to participate in good writing. Not just listeners, but reactionaries. And these reactionaries share a common cause for their reactions but often not the same reactions. Question and answer sessions often follow author's readings and the author may point to intended meanings and effects to assist and encourage understanding, but the author may not even be fully aware of all that he or she has accomplished and there is not a single "correct" reaction. There is, however, a singular sense of engagement. The reader responds to the writer first and foremost, not to the other readers. The writer's audience can be a million people, but one at a time.

Who, then, are you writing for? The answer might seem obvious. For example, in a beginning college composition course, you are, of course, writing to please the instructor. Yes, you are, but it's not that simple. Your instructor is not likely to be pleased by writing that merely mimics lectures and suggestions. You must take this information in and process it, apply it, in your own way. You can attempt to consider your audience (and learn from that consideration) as a writer on assignment for a particular magazine or newspaper might consider its subscribers. You can be careful not to "talk down" to your readers or confuse them unnecessarily. And yet the most important audience you have is yourself. If the writing doesn't engage you, it certainly won't interest the reader.

Your reader can be assumed to put up with a lot, at least for a while, just as any audience wants to encourage a speaker, as long as the speaker stays interesting. You can appeal to emotions, to reasoning, to fears, to human curiosity and the natural desire to be entertained. You don't know any details about the reader's character, but you do know the reader has the same emotional and thinking apparatus you have, and you should assume the reader is at least as intelligent and capable as you are, unless you know for certain that a particular limited audience will be reading your writing. Even when writing for such an audience, it is better to challenge them than to bore them. A children's book, for example, that aims at a less educated and experienced audience, is just that much better and more enduring if it interests adults as well as reaches (and challenges) younger readers. This is not the primary purpose, and if it doesn't accomplish its primary purpose of reaching the children, the game is lost, but good writing emerges from many unexpected sources by recognizing and encouraging the larger human values and questions in any subject that interest us all. Do you remember that book you read as a child that you didn't quite understand but it captivated your attention *and* made you return to it as you got older?

Let the reader look over your shoulder as you involve and entertain the audience of yourself. Excitement and interest are intoxicating. Start with your own and let them spread. You are writing for yourself and you are going to learn something in the process. That should keep you excited and encouraged with the prospect of something new. In this way, you will be using the same purpose the reader has for reading to motivate you in your writing. This mutual purpose, acknowledged, creates a bond. Like you, the reader is always looking for something new. And it's the searching for it that matters the most. Enjoy the adventure enough and part of the treasure is already found.

Manipulation

Is writing a game? Writing is certainly not unimportant, but there is an element of game playing in all writing. Good writing is the art of manipulation. The writer is always testing to see what he can get away with. You are, after all, coaxing the reader to follow you, overcoming the reader's inertia. Why should he or she read this? If the reader's reason for paying (yes, you are selling something, your viewpoint) attention is for information only, much of the power of effective writing is lost. If all writing is manipulation, then two types of manipulation can be seen. Obvious manipulation creates resistance in any situation, written or not, but subtle, organized, intelligent, unique maneuvering is a kind of coaxing towards the writer's goals that the reader not only accepts but encourages. Readers are willing to be led, but they do need a reason to follow. It doesn't even have to be a very good reason, but it must be an interesting one. Good writers recognize this and encourage readers to follow by providing an interesting trail of suggestive, thought-provoking clues. The experience of being manipulated by a careful, considerate and lively writer becomes an exchange, a dialogue about the life in the writer's mind as he or she weaves a fascinating pattern for us, a shared discovery. Manipulation of a more obvious sort is only another tired argument that isn't going anywhere and nobody likes a one-sided conversation. Be sure to include both sides of the discussion. Life exists in tension and conflict and writing should be alive.

Your audience, then, contains a wide range of interested personalities willing to be manipulated if you give them a good reason. They are not dumb, just willing. They are perceptive about weaknesses and flaws, but they are forgiving, if they perceive care and thought. They are alive, responsive. They are patient, but not merely passive. They are open to new ideas and new ways of expressing old ideas. They enjoy the unexpected, but they want it to lead somewhere. And they are all these things because they are you.

Writing and Reading

Writing is an applied skill. No amount of textbook memorization or reading can teach you how to do it. You have to write and rewrite, think and rethink, to make your writing anything more than simple conveyance of information, and even that is not easy. Once you are actively involved in writing, frequent, thoughtful reading can teach a lot. Where one might want to go and why it's worth the trip is likely to be discovered only from the best accounts of what's there by other travellers. But you need to read differently than you might read for information only.

Much of the reading most people do is skimming for factual information. The writing that carries the facts is of little additional value. It is unfortunate that our need for factual information has encouraged so much publication of writing that exists only to contain the facts because facts can only have their full importance and meaning when they are interpreted. How information is revealed can be as meaningful as what is revealed. Writing worth more careful consideration contains a wealth of suggestive and implied meaning that creates a personality (style) and we begin to react to the writing as well as the information. Just as the same speech makes two different impressions when handled by two different speakers, thoughtful and carefully rewritten and shaped writing is not just a matter of being "correct" or even "clear" but a search for meaning and an attempt to be engaging. Thoughtful reading has much to teach if only you will slow down, consider and enjoy how the information is delivered rather than merely what facts are presented.

Good writing will often encourage you to slow down. It may give you pleasure in the reading, stimulate your curiosity, or make you think. This is much more than entertainment, especially to someone learning to write. A good writer can make it all seem deceptively simple, but if you begin to ask how it was done and try to do it yourself, you can learn a tremendous amount from the dialogue of questioning and considering that will occur as you read. But you will need to be actively trying to write well yourself before the questions that can help you learn the most from your reading will even occur to you. Many of these questions are very individual and there can be no definitive list of useful questions for a beginning writer to ask of what he or she reads, but you can begin by asking questions about the relationship between the writer's manner of presentation and the subject. Good writers vary how they say it to suit each new subject and purpose.

We're all different. That is the great problem and the most exciting challenge and opportunity in writing. We all have different kinds of problems particular to each new subject each time we write. And although there are many useful guidelines to consider that can help you write well, each writer's answer to any one set of problems will and should reflect the writer's individuality. But how can we recognize it when we haven't read much to compare it to? And how can we develop it if we're not clear how it's different? It is that difference which is finally what any writer has to offer that can interest all of us. And how can you know if you've found your own way if you haven't experienced the ways of others?

II. The Major Elements of Writing

Point of View

Among the first choices a writer makes, sometimes impulsively or even unconsciously, point of view may be the element out of which the other elements emerge. Point of view has two different, but related meanings. It is, of course, a matter of one's opinions or perspective on the subject, but to a writer, it is also, in a more concrete way, a matter of which pronoun the author uses to address the subject. Whether the author is choosing to speak in first person, third person, or (less likely) second person affects the assumptions and expectations of both the reader and the author. These assumptions are only tendencies, not true limits. For example, when the writing is in first person, it would commonly be assumed that the perspective will be more personal, more directly involved with the speaker, that the psychic distance between the voice and the subject will be less. Yet it is possible to write in first person and create exactly the opposite effect. Just as it is possible to write in third person in a manner that creates an impression of immediacy and personal connection. The writer should not merely ignore the reader's expectations, but he or she may choose to defy them if the purpose becomes apparent in the writing.

And point of view is not merely a matter of choosing a pronoun. The writer can choose to speak for animals, objects, or even ideas, giving a voice to that which does not ordinarily have one.

Once a point of view is chosen, it may be changed using an appropriately clear transition. Multiple points of view can often help give a more complete understanding of the subject and its meanings. Be sure to pay careful attention to the transitions from one point of view to another when using multiple points of view.

Some authors choose to begin with a point of view which is later shown to be a different one than it first appeared to be. For example, a first person point of view may not immediately use "I." It may at first seem objective but gradually become more personal and finally reveal the "I" speaker. If the reason this speaker has had to approach the subject from a distance before becoming more intimate with it has become obvious, the strategy may work very well.

There are two ways to explore the possibilities of various points of view. The writer can think through the strategy to be used on the subject and plan out the sequence of uses of points of view first (plot the sequence), or the writer can simply begin writing with no clear concept of the organization to be used, searching for it as clues emerge from the initial attempts to grapple with the subject's meaning. The latter can be a very productive method but requires patience and a bit of detective work. The writer should notice unusual moments and choices in the writing when it's time for revision work (don't trip over your shoelaces by getting too involved in editing while creating). If, as many writers suggest, the other elements of writing often emerge from the choice of point of view, then backtracking is also possible; clues to how point of view can best serve the writing exist in thoughtful questioning of how the other elements (style, uses of character, choice of structure, etc.) are linked to it. The writer's ultimate goal is to make all the elements of the writing work together, so questioning their relationships as you revise is a productive way to develop the work. It would be advisable to be able to work in both approaches, rather than to limit yourself to just one way of writing.

Point of view can also be used to make discoveries about the subject. Unexpected realizations can occur when a point of view is attempted that is not the author's usual approach. Useful contrasts can be achieved when the point of view is a less familiar one. It's all the author's point of view in the sense that it represents the way the author sees it, of course, but the presentation can create the appearance of variety and perspective and help give depth to the subject. Varying the use of point of view can take both the reader's and the writer's psychology to new recognitions about the subject, surprises that enliven the work and create freshness and originality.

Style

All writing reveals the character behind the voice to some degree. The style does not need to contain any direct information at all to provide "personality" assumptions to the reader which the reader may not even realize have occurred. Attitude, sense of humor, implications of judgment, suggestions of degree of experience, level of diction, syntax, tone and other aspects of style too numerous to detail all provide the reader with clues to the background of the character to whom the voice belongs. In nonfiction, there is a degree of expectation that, unless clearly directed otherwise, the voice belongs more literally to the author than one would assume in fiction. This can be deliberately redirected to create a character who is not the author speaking, just as in fiction, but the author is much more likely in nonfiction than in fiction to use him or her self literally as the primary character voice.

Think about the various levels on which this "character" is revealed. The level of word choice (diction) used by the voice points to the degree of education and knowledge and the context of the character's experience, the "world" from which the character derives his or her use of words. And as the words chosen are placed in sequence in sentences, another level of knowledge of character emerges for the reader as phrases and sentence structures (syntax) reveal more about the character's world. As the implications multiply, the reader forms a more and more complex impression of the person behind the voice, including motive, reliability, complexity and intelligence. The thoughtful writer will, therefore, consider the clues he or she is providing to these elements and use them to lead the reader in a constructive direction that will assist in revealing the point of the essay.

As with point of view, variation of style can also be used to create contrast, complexity and depth of understanding if effective transitions between the styles are provided. An author might choose, for example, to contrast characters from different "worlds" by revealing them through their styles of expression as well as their points of view.

Consider this short anecdote:

A man and a woman are arguing in a restaurant. A small dog appears and sits patiently next to the woman, who hasn't noticed the dog. The waiter begins talking to an elderly gentleman sitting at a table by himself, gesturing towards the man and woman. The man tosses a glass of wine on the woman, picks up the dog and leaves the restaurant, getting into a Lexus with a personalized license plate that reads "NOT ME."

Try exploring the meaning of this scene using the different voices and styles of witnesses or involved parties such as:

1. an evangelist who has come here for the first time
2. an off-duty policeman who is tired and hungry
3. a young man with his date who has suddenly realized he cannot pay for the meal
4. a woman eating alone who is considering divorce
5. the owner of the restaurant
6. the owner of the rusted-out Buick parked behind the man's Lexus
7. an escaped convict who has been living under an assumed name for twenty years
8. a transvestite who has thus far in the evening gone unnoticed
9. a teenager having dinner with her parents
10. the chemist responsible for the invention of latex
11. a writer spending his first royalty check
12. a grandmother with thirty-two grandchildren
13. a circus performer
14. a cockroach hiding in a crack of the table

15. an ordinary middle-aged man who has discovered
    he has cancer
16. the wine steward's gay lover
17. the boy scouts walking by on their way to a pancake
    dinner
18. the wine glass

Try adding more characters to the list. Consider the possibilities of using more than one point of view.

Even a single "character" can be presented with different styles, including the contrast between the character's moments of objectivity and moments of immediate subjective response. How would you feel at the time? How would you feel later, after you've had time to think about it? Changes over time in the way a character has learned to express what was once more immediate and less understood often occur in writing about your own experience (memoir).

Try writing about something that happened to you long ago. When you're finished, write about it again, pretending no time at all has elapsed, that it's happening even as you write. Compare the two styles.

A character, such as yourself, might think in a different manner than he or she speaks, or speak in a different manner than he or she writes, and these contrasts can work in the same way that multiple characters or points of view can. Italics are sometimes used to reflect these differences.

Try speaking your work into a tape recorder and transcribing it into written form. Compare this style to the one you use when you write rather than speak your meanings. You may discover that you already have two different voices. Now try it again, thinking about who you are speaking to, and change the person addressed a few times. Each time you do this you are likely to create a somewhat different style or voice. This is a simple equivalent to what the writer can do in writ-

45

ten form to contrast the manner in which he or she addresses the reader.

Style can also be used to suggest and imply meaning. It is especially effective when the reader understands something through suggestive language that does not need to be stated. More meaning with fewer words, the effect of a poet, has the added advantage of honoring the reader's intelligence and attentiveness. What reader doesn't like feeling clever from understanding something that wasn't actually stated?

Among the most elusive and important words used to talk about style, tone can be the hardest to understand. It is so important because it is a way of talking about information the reader receives from the writing indirectly, through implication. A master of these stylistic clues can make us think the writer is someone the writer is not. In essays, these clues may be kept to a minimum in order to appear to be "objective" and to focus attention on the subject more than on the writer's or the character's personality, but even in journalistic or technical writing, the reader tends to acquire an impression of the kind of person who has written what he is reading, even if that person is primarily defined by his "objective" stance.

The potential for carefully controlling information given by the way the author writes, rather than only by what he says, is nearly unlimited and in its extreme the author can even imply that he is in total disagreement with what he appears to be saying, as in satire.

There is no magic list of the effects that can be achieved by tone, but writers can add further control to tonal effects by comparing their writing quirks and tendencies to those of other authors and considering what readers might tend to assume from them. Try describing the appearance of a writer based on an essay in which the author does not describe him or her self. Try drawing a picture of the author. Ask several people to do this. Chances are, there will be a surprising similarity based only on implication and suggestion in the writing. A good writer tries to identify the unique characteristics of his use of language and develop them. Try naming some of those used in the author's essay which helped to make the drawings. Refer to the other major elements of writing and question their relationships to help identify the author's tone. What are the most unique elements of the essay?

Now try to establish an initial list of your own writing tendencies. What do you as a writer do differently from other writers? Is there a way to make these differences support what you want to say about your subject? As you read essays, think about what the author's style tells you about who the author is and what the author thinks. Do you find you form presumptions about what the author might think concerning subjects other than those the author has addressed directly in the essay? However quiet and subtle, do you find you have developed a sense of who this person is? Now think about how much could be accomplished if this writer knew you would do this and deliberately controlled the information about the author that appeared in this seemingly accidental way. Good writers know good readers will do this, and they use the reader's involvement in this process to help them say what they want to say.

There are several devices that can assist you in clarifying style variations by making the transitions between styles more apparent. One of the more conspicuous is the use of italics. This alerts the reader visually to the difference in the voice. Quotes can also serve this purpose, but they do so with the reader's expectation that the words are actually uttered or at least thought in verbalized form. Space transitions can be used to change styles or "voices" and if a clear sequence is established, a pattern can also alert the reader to which voice is being presented without any other direct clues. Numbering or naming sections can assist with this effect.

Organization

Plot is a fiction writer's approach to sequence. A writer of nonfiction can use sequence in all the ways a fiction writer does, but it's usually better to think in broader terms so as not to limit the possibilities of creative nonfiction to fiction's viewpoint. Patterns of thinking are more likely to be the essay writer's organizational approach and plot can be thought of as merely one of those patterns, most literally applied in narrative. Some of the most frequently applied patterns are covered in section III on rhetorical modes. For an essay writer, these patterns of thinking function mostly in the development portion of the essay, the larger middle "body" of the essay.

Organization exists on many levels in any written expression. Each sentence has its own organization. But often it is the organization of the larger units, the paragraphs and the work as a whole, that determines what will work well in the sentences. Whether you start from the sentence or from the essay as a whole, the parts need to carry a useful relationship to each other. Sentences and paragraphs do not work in isolation.

The patterns of thinking in section III and the discussion of the three basic parts of an essay in this section will help with larger organizational concepts, but two basic possibilities must be considered as well. Should you present your idea followed by supporting detail or should you use supporting detail to lead to your idea? This operates in a paragraph, a section, or a whole essay. Generally speaking, the more difficult, argumentative, or disagreeable the idea is, the more likely supporting detail should guide the reader to it instead of follow a statement of it. But you should always consider both possibilities and you should also remember the value of variety. A good writer doesn't let habit lead the writing when choice could drive it.

The three basic parts of an essay have been described in numerous ways and have been endlessly analyzed because they contain endless possibilities or they would not be so useful. We can call them introduction, development, and conclusion or initiation, consequence, and denouement or thesis, support, and resolution or a hundred other variations. Or we can simply call them beginning, middle, and end. The terminology matters little, but on the most basic level, organization is a recognition of the natural laws of physics and motion. Whether it's motion or reader involvement in an essay, there are three movements required to complete an act and each requires something different—you have to get started, you have to keep going and you have to stop. Just as our lives consist of birth, life and death. It's really that simple to understand the parts, but it requires careful attention to successfully move from one to another at an effectively chosen moment. The confusion results from the failure to successfully shift gears.

A writer's earliest introductions to these organizational parts is likely to prescribe a highly organized, but very boring, format in which the thesis sentence states the central idea, the development supports and details it and the conclusion summarizes it. This is often presented as the five paragraph essay with one paragraph for the introduction, three paragraphs for the development and one paragraph for the conclusion. While this is clearly organized, it is also telling us what you're going to do, doing it, and then telling us what you already did—not very interesting and obviously repetitive. Three part organization does not have to mean repeating yourself.

There are many effective organizational methods. The useful ways of organizing ultimately can be as complex as the human mind itself. But the writer cannot expect the reader to follow complex organization without assistance. This assistance does not need to be obvious and can be provided in the form of many other, sometimes very subtle, writing devices, including symbolism, verb tense relationships, implied meaning, dialogue, foreshadowing, transitional aids, etc. To be effective, the writer is often making careful decisions about the differences between unnecessary and self-evident "guidance" (sometimes seen as clear, but tediously boring, organization) and enriching patterns that add dimension to the meaning of the writing. Ability at making such decisions well comes from enough practice in attempting them to understand the problems and enough thoughtful reading to be exposed to the possibilities. The best answer to the problem is unique to each new subject and writer, but learning writers must be sensitive to discovering possibilities and willing to thoughtfully attempt variations while critically questioning the results. A good developing writer, then, is a writer who is confident and adventurous in attempting the unknown and thoughtful in evaluating and rewriting following the freedom of the attempt.

A good writer is really a master of two different skills, writing and editing. He is an adventurous explorer of verbal possibility first, and then, after he has returned from the adventure, he is a constructive, but unrelenting, critic of the record he has made of his journey. Both skills are valuable even by themselves, but together they create a consistently fascinating, clear, and developing writer. The difficulty is that these are two very different skills. It may help to imagine yourself as literally two different people when you are first performing these skills. Some writers even go so far as to dress differently or wear a different hat to put them in a different frame of mind when shifting these gears. Visualize the difference between the two modes of thinking if you can. Practice keeping them separate. The time may come when you can move back and forth between them quickly, but they are two different ways of aiding your writing and you should begin by treating them as very different skills that may conflict with one

51

another if you try to perform them at the same time. The thinking it takes to be a good editor is not the same as the thinking it takes to be a good writer. Let these two distinctly different skills develop separately first before you try to bring them together and even then, be prepared to separate them when they confuse each other.

Outlines

An outline is only a guess, a possible route to an uncertain treasure, and any good explorer knows it may be necessary to get there by a different route. But it often helps to have a map when you start, even if you decide to go after a different treasure in mid-adventure. Treat it informally, a Mr. Potato Head you can keep moving parts on until you have the "character" you want.

Don't let an outline turn you away from the useful surprises that happen during the actual writing. Doing an outline is a function of your critic personality and this "organizer" personality should not be present when the more subconscious creator is at work. Learn to trust your instincts when you're writing and look in the critic's mirror only when your creator has decided it's time to take a break. Nurture a mutual respect between these two aspects of your writing, but don't forget that they are different functions. Letting an outline control you, rather than suggest possible direction, is like missing the scenery because you're worried about what time you're going to get there. Don't look at the map unless you're lost.

Introductions

The first job an essay writer has is to get the reader's attention. This can be done in numerous ways, including even jokes, radical styles, alternate voices, dreams, mystery, etc. The choice of introduction should, however, help draw the reader into the development as well as get the reader's attention. The introduction may also be used to connect to the conclusion, to provide an additional structure, a "frame," for the essay.

Don't forget that the introduction does not need to be written first. If you don't have a good idea, move on and return to it later. Sometimes the best introduction won't be apparent until the structure of the rest of the essay is emerging. And don't let the name fool you. To introduce is not, for an essay writer, simply to tell the reader what you're going to do. It means making the reader interested. It may even mean tricking the reader. But it must, most of all, mean getting the reader's attention. Convince the reader you're going to be interesting, worthy of the investment of energy and thought.

Developments

The development is where most of the essay's detail is presented to back up and demonstrate its point. Because it is the longest part of the essay, it may also have greater need of further organization, beyond the needs of the rest of the essay. This is usually where the rhetorical modes assist the essay in patterning the information and also where variety of approach can supply greater dimension. This is where you can't remind yourself enough to, "Show us; don't tell us." Take your time, especially on the first draft and, "Be specific." Overabundance of detail can be corrected in revision much easier than lack of it. Too much detail simply makes it easier to see which details are working best.

Since the writer is working towards a conclusion, there may be a tendency to let the destination overpower the journey. Don't forget that the reader needs to share the experiences that led you to the conclusion before the full impact and importance of the conclusion can be appreciated. To put it in terms of the birth, life, death sequence, be sure to enjoy the life fully before performing the autopsy.

Conclusions

Summary is often thought of as an effective conclusion and it may well be so, if the summary does not merely repeat the most important elements of the development. But why not add to this or provide an even more effective statement or perspective on the point? Summary needs special attention to its phrasing and manner of presentation because it always risks being perceived as merely repetition.

A good conclusion is frequently the most difficult part of an essay. Not only must you shift gears to accomplish a feeling of completion for the reader, you must also complete and connect any parts of the essay which may have appeared unrelated. If you began with a point in mind, you may well have accomplished this while writing, but that approach risks predictability and potential boredom. If you discovered your point while writing, that discovery may fascinate the reader, but you will probably have to edit out some warm-up material. Each approach has its possibilities and its dangers.

A good conclusion is often made effective by careful attention to the phrasing and emphasis of how it is written. A good conclusion may also extend the point of the essay rather than simply state it. It can do this by providing an especially effective example that can stand for a final statement of the importance and clarity of the point. It can do this by applying the conclusion to other circumstances, subjects or characters to show the true extent of its importance. It can do this by changing the context in which the point is seen to show how it may be applied.

Whatever else your conclusion does, it is the last possibility you have to accomplish your purposes. This is not the time to throw in something overlooked or to get defensive or apologetic. The conclusion should move on from and naturally extend what you have presented in the development. It needs to contain your best writing and most effective statements. Merely repeating what you have already written is not enough.

Some Types of Conclusions

1. Although merely repeating is not sufficient, there are complicated essay structures which can benefit from a brief refresher that brings wide-ranging ideas back together. The key to making this type of conclusion work is to say it so freshly that it does not appear to be a repetition.

2. Demonstrate and enhance your point with a dramatic example.

3. Ask a question. Be sure it's a question which your essay has already given the reader adequate information to think about constructively. This often works as a suggestion of one or more of the implications of the point. It should extend the meaning of your essay, not merely repeat one of its topics.

4. Apply your point to the future. Suggest what will happen as a result of the point you have made.

5. Use your best and clearest example to clarify the point so that it doesn't need to be stated or can be stated in a more unexpected way.

6. Use an example that combines several different elements of your presentation, thus making the organization feel complete.

7. Circle back to the opening of your essay. If you have successfully given a clearer understanding of something presented there, this return can make your essay feel satisfying and complete.

8. Use the conclusion to start a new cycle of meaning similar to the one your essay has covered, implying that this cycle too will come out the way you have described. The end is often really a beginning, a new beginning for an essay the writer has sparked in the reader's head.

Transitions

As the parts of the essay become clearer and you can see that an essay does not simply flow from one part to another, but rather, is built, constructed from sections and pieces, it also becomes clearer that these parts must be fitted together. The glue that provides unity to them is created by effective use of transitions.

The most obvious transitions are provided by word clues, often words suggesting the passage of time or the relationship in time of one section to another. There are innumerable words and phrases that can provide these transitions, but the writer should become aware of the ones he most frequently uses. Good transitions are made by choice, not habit. If you can see that you have a tendency to create transitions with certain oft-repeated words, it's time to expand your repertoire. Begin by trying it without the key time words. Often a transition can be achieved simply by recognizing where it needs to occur and providing a non-word clue to the shift it represents.

Paragraphing is the most obvious non-word transition aid. Often the recognition of a new train of thought or aspect to the subject which can be provided by a new paragraph is enough to provide an adequate transition.

If the transition is larger than a paragraph can smoothly bridge, consider a space transition. Perhaps all that is needed is a pause (a line of white space in the text) to allow the reader to reorient and consider the new section freshly, aware that some of the writing's elements may change following the visual pause. If space transitions are also used to create a pattern, this provides additional clues to the elements of the writing which might be changing at each space transition.

If space transitions have already been used or if the transition is very large, asterisks can be added to show a greater shift. If still larger transitions are needed, numbering or section titles can provide the transition.

To practice transitions and to discover how well they can work, try this experiment:

1. Start with ten or twelve unrelated pieces of writing, a paragraph or two each. Try this with ten or twelve different writers for the most extreme challenge.

2. Now create at least three different sequences for these pieces, trying to suggest they were deliberately written this way to make a point.

3. Now try different transitions, allowing yourself only a few words for each transition or none at all.

4. Finally, allow yourself one final section of about the same length to use for a conclusion if your three pieces do not yet seem completed.

5. Use a title that suggests how the variety of styles is being used to make your point if it still seems unclear.

Whatever methods of transition you choose, try not to use the same ones all the time. Good writers are always attempting to enlarge their bag of tricks.

Titles

A title is not merely a label. It can provide an added dimension or perspective. It can draw attention to an important, but perhaps less obvious, aspect of the essay. It can serve the function of an introduction (get the reader's attention) or even the conclusion. It can surprise or create further understanding. It can provide humor. It can be a question or a statement or a phrase or only a word. But it is not merely a label. If you have a glass jar of peaches, it doesn't help much to write "peaches" on the label.

Sometimes in class I have placed my crumpled coat on the table, told the class it was a sculpture and asked them to create at least three different titles for it. Try this for yourself. Any object will do, but don't make it too easy to name. If you're doing this in a group, compare the variety of types of titles that are created and consider what each type could do for an essay. If you're doing this alone, create at least a dozen different titles. Find an anthology of contemporary poetry and browse through the list of titles for more types.

Some Types of Titles

1. Use a phrase from the essay that takes on a new meaning when seen out of context.

2. Treat the essay as a metaphor. A title can suggest that the real subject is different from the apparent one, that your essay is really an example used to demonstrate a point that applies to other subjects.

3. Opposites. Try labeling your essay with the opposite of what it's about to suggest contrast and irony. This may give more dimension to your point.

4. Use your title as the introduction. The title may read right into the first line of the essay or it may serve the introduction's purpose of getting the reader's attention.

5. Point to a less obvious meaning of your essay with the title. This can expand the impact and applications of your point.

6. Contrasting styles. Use a phrasing in the title markedly different from the style used in the body of the essay. This can suggest the relationship of your point to the type of person who would use the title's phrasing, to another point of view.

7. Allusion. Use your title to suggest a connection to a well-known work which has something related to say about your point. This is often done with an epigraph, but can also be done with a title.

8. Make a statement. A title can be a complete sentence. It can therefore provoke and raise curiosity as well as create a sense of confidence. A title need not be a fragment.

9. Conclusion. A title can be the conclusion of the essay. This works well when the relationship of the title to the development is not at first obvious and using the conclusion in the title does not give everything away. The reader's reaction at the end of the essay should be, "Now I see what that title meant." This title's first function is to raise curiosity about the essay. It then, later, has a different meaning, often a more ironic one, than the one it first appeared to have. It sounds complicated, but it's not hard to do. We begin an essay as innocents. We end having had an experience, an understanding. A title can have different meanings from these two perspectives.

Remember, a title should add to your essay. It can serve more than one of the functions suggested and this is by no means an exhaustive list. There are many more ways in which a title can function to add something to your essay. It should not be merely an afterthought.

Try experimenting with several different titles on your essay and then select the one that works best. Don't settle for the first one that comes to you. It's likely to be merely the most obvious.

Character

Character is always present in writing, even in seemingly objective nonfiction, although it may be deliberately moved behind other effects and considerations. Even when the approach is relatively objective, it can be useful to use the "character" of others through quotes and differing viewpoints to clarify your purposes. Don't forget that the way people say something often carries more meaning than what they say. It may even contradict what they say. Good quotes often carry multiple meanings and implications. More meaning with fewer words is useful. It can assist the writer in moving closer to showing meaning, so that telling or explaining it isn't necessary.

Even when characters are not unique but created as deliberate stereotypes, let them have enough room and specific detail to establish their reality in the essay. The effect of a deliberate stereotype is not lost by making the character more "real."

And if one character speaking is effective, think what two or more speaking in different ways with different opinions can do. Dialogue allows the nonfiction writer to "tell the truth" of what was said while borrowing the "fiction" writer's techniques of both narrative (sequence) and characterization. It also provides contrast to the writer's own voice or "persona," which is also a character.

Letting characters talk about each other helps to "round" the characters. It makes them more alive. And it does this even if they are imaginary.

Providing enough "rounding" or detail for characters also helps avoid the problem of sentimentality. Sentiment, what I would call "earned" emotion, achieved through sufficient detail to make the reader respond emotionally, gives power to the writing. Sentimentality, or "unearned" emotion, weakens it. If you simply tell your reader how someone felt, the reader doesn't know if they really would share the emotion or not and the effect is sentimentality, a cheapening of emotional impact and meaning, a kind of lie about the emotions involved. If we believe emotions are important and want to make a statement about them, we should realize that we have an obligation to create them for the reader, not merely ask for them. Crying isn't enough. The reader must experience the things that caused the crying. Otherwise, it's just whining. Don't dismiss the emotional impact of your writing by merely labeling emotion. Make the reader live through what caused it. Create emotional responses. Don't just ask for them.

While it might sound artificial, it also often works to apply these same possibilities to nonhuman "characters." This is called personification. As long as it is not overdone to the point of silliness (unless for humorous effect), this can add a dimension of emotional engagement with the nonhuman "character." As long as it contributes to the essay's point, it will be accepted by the reader as a surprising and useful way to understand the essay.

Theme

All art has themes. In an essay, the reader's expectation is usually that theme will be more directly and clearly a controlling device for the organization and presentation of the writing than in other art forms. Although contemporary creative essay writing grants freedoms often not expected in traditional academic essays, a more literal kind of "truth" generally functions in some way to help create the effects unique to nonfiction. Otherwise the author would have chosen to present the work as fiction. This function may serve to create little more than the *appearance* of a literal "truth" used to find or create a deeper, less factual, "truth," but it encourages the reader to question why this information is being presented. This question is usually kept far back in the mind when reading fiction because the first concern is simply engagement, the creation of an alternative world or experience for which the demand of any literal "reality" is secondary, if it exists at all. The presence in an essay of this implied "why" is used by the writer of nonfiction in the same way that "What happens next?" is often used by the writer of fiction, to organize the work. And so it becomes helpful to think of themes in essay writing as "points." A theme, then, becomes a more specific, and usually more direct, use of a point in an essay.

This does not mean that the creative writer has to fall back on the simplistic statement of thesis sentences and the obvious organizational pattern of the five paragraph essay, that well organized and usually boring monolith of high school English classes, but it does suggest that a clear statement of point or points would be a useful thing to have at hand while revising and shaping the work. So much the better if the point becomes clear without needing statement, but this is not likely to happen merely by accident. Often the point is gradually shaped into clarity, through revision, from a kernel of a suggestion noticed and developed throughout several drafts of the work.

It has been said that there are really very few themes in writing, maybe even only life and death, and that it's all been said before. Even if a writer were to believe this to be true, it does not negate the reason for writing. And nouns like "life" and "death" are not really points but subjects. Points are full sentences, statements of meaning, not simply nouns. A couple of important nouns can provide the basis for a virtually unlimited quantity of engaging statements and therefore, an unlimited quantity of points to make in essays. The basic truths of human life are not easy to understand and even if they have been written before, they have not been written in your way. Your way of saying it may be the way that opens up understanding for the reader that did not exist when the same thing was said by another writer. The great truths must continually be rediscovered.

III. Patterns of Thought

Rhetoric

Yes, it's a strange word and it can look very intimidating. Why might a secction of a book on writing be organized according to rhetorical structures? It's really much simpler than it looks. Rhetoric is about how we think and therefore how we write. Ultimately, if we are as intelligent as most of us would like to believe, our thought processes are almost unbelievably complicated, and yet for all that complexity, we seem to manage to explain ourselves to each other. We manage this by creating and developing patterns. This section will explore several of the most useful patterns and point out some of the numerous ways of combining and extending them. Keep in mind that useful patterns are nearly endless. The patterns covered here are merely the most commonly used. When we say, of a politician, for example, that his speech was "all rhetoric," we are saying we recognize the logic of its patterns, but it contained no substance. Many beginning writers have the opposite problem, substance without an effective pattern of presentation.

In exploring these patterns, do not underestimate the reader's ability to recognize and follow them. Subtle connections can be effective and no reader likes the feeling of overexplanation, of being "talked down to."

Rhetoric is a means of achieving a dialogue. Writing is a bridge between two human beings and rhetoric is the structure of that bridge. The more we can understand about how it is built, the more certain our steps can be. We can admire the river instead of worrying about falling into it.

Sensation:
How Do We Experience the World?

Two important pieces of advice are likely to be heard repeatedly in beginning writing classes: 1) Show us; don't tell us. 2) Be specific. Why this nagging insistence on detail and demonstration? It can help to start by trying to think of how human beings make sense of their world. The reasons for this insistence are not based on "rules" or the eccentricities and peculiar interests of writing teachers.

As a child, you learned to see, smell, touch, hear and taste first. Then you made gradually increasing "sense" out of this sensual input (notice the relationship of "sense" to "sensual"). This was not just child's play. As adults we still learn in much the same way.

Try this:

1. Get two or more friends and two bags.

2. Place some things in the bags that will not be easily named.

3. Let each friend reach into one of the bags and touch, smell, anything except look.

4. Ask each friend to write with two purposes in mind. Describe what's in the bag and maintain the reader's interest.

5. Ask each friend to read the result, using another friend, who had a different bag, as the audience.

6. How well did the writer achieve the two purposes? Which purpose did the writer seem to focus the most on? Which purpose was most important to the listener (reader)? Was the description accurate enough for the

listener to actually draw pictures of the subjects? How much does the listener care about accuracy?

7. Reverse positions until each of you has had a chance to write and listen in this way.

8. Discuss your reliance on sight to describe. Which other sense were you most comfortable using? Which was the most unfamiliar to apply in your writing?

9. What would you do differently now that you have this information from both readers and other writers? Did your experience as the listener alter your focus as the writer?

Reading what "sense" someone made of their sensory input can be interesting, but it is much more interesting to be able to experience the particular events that led them to their conclusions. As readers we want the life (sensory input) itself. If the detail is presented carefully, the readers will share the same conclusions from it that the writer did or at least will have all the information necessary to make up their own minds. You can lead them down the right path, but not until the path itself has been created. Even if they disagree with the writer's conclusions, they are thinking about the subject with more of the writer's experience (walking the same path), and this kind of involved disagreement is far better than the great enemy of all writers, boredom. As sensitive readers (and all readers are more "sensitive" than many writers think) we want the life, not the eulogy.

Description

The universal is achieved through the specific. Detail provides the specifics that allow the writer to support and give meaning to larger statements. Before we can reach effective conclusions, we must supply the evidence that led us to them. We do this with detailed sense-based description.

Show us. Don't tell us. It's the most common advice given to writers and with good reason. It sounds simple, but it applies in so many different ways that a writer can spend a lifetime discovering how many different possibilities are covered by this seemingly simple advice. It's the basis of how we learn about our world from the very moment of birth. We learn from experience, not just explanation. Recreate the experience with detail and thoughtful description. Let us experience the meaning. Then we will respond more fully, and we will remember our response as we remember the important events of our lives, with our senses.

In writing you are dealing with a universe of symbols. Words themselves are symbols. There is a degree of generality already inherent in using words because they apply to multiple situations. They have to. But some words do this more than others. The more general the word choice is, then, the more meanings it may contain for the readers. This may sound like an advantage, but it's not. Instead of applying more widely to readers, it means that it is more widely scattered in its meaning and therefore, less clear. Through being more concrete instead, more specific in word choice, the writer achieves greater understanding, a more universal recognition of the applications of his or her meaning.

Don't worry about the broader meanings of your work until after you have created your specific ones. Create clarity first, with thoughtfully chosen specific detail. Apply the created clarity, if needed, later.

Be specific. Then be more specific. Then be even more specific. Particularly on the first draft, err towards too much and too specific detail. It is much easier to edit out the excess than it is to recreate the moment and insert more.

As an exercise, much like an artist would, go somewhere and draw. In words. Experience a simple, ordinary location fully. Try to describe it in specific detail, just as an artist would have to translate visual impressions into line and shape. Use words as if they were physical things. Use the words that carry the most sense impressions and keep them as specific as you can.

It might seem obvious that good writing must consist of detail, but one of the most common difficulties for all writers is recognizing when the writing has not been specific enough. A writer must use his senses to help the reader understand, through detail, the writer's intentions. It is not enough to tell the reader about something. If the writer expects an important reaction from the reader, he must re-*create* what led him to his views, his conclusions. Without specific concrete details, the reader has no basis for trusting the evidence that the writer has used in developing his attitudes.

An inexperienced writer often uses abstract language that makes it more difficult to say exactly what he means. Abstract words represent ideas, concepts, etc. which may have a wide range of meanings and responses for the reader. Words like "love" and "God," for example, contain such a large number of meanings that each reader may interpret their meaning a little differently. Abstract words can, of course, serve very useful purposes in writing, but beginning writers tend to use them with their own specific meaning in mind, not realizing that the reader may be thinking of quite a different meaning.

It is usually easier to be specific with concrete words, especially ones that call upon the responses of the reader's senses. Concrete words are the physical ones, the ones that appeal to our five senses, the ones without so many different possible interpretations. "Concrete" is a concrete word.

Detail, then, is needed to bridge the gap between reader and writer in nearly all forms of writing, and it is often useful to convey detail with the senses, in concrete language. But there is a tremendous amount of detail that could be written about nearly any subject. Once focused clearly on providing useful detail, it quickly becomes apparent to the writer that some selectivity is needed. The good writer identifies the "revealing" details because they allow him to say more with fewer words. A good writer is also a good observer. Human beings are bombarded daily with a staggering amount of information and for our very survival, we learn to screen this information, to notice only that which has changed, for example. A good writer will become aware of this and notice, again, what most of us have taught ourselves to overlook, and further, will learn to look at the world from new angles which are often not really new at all, just forgotten. John Keats said it is the job of the poet to find similarities in dissimilar things. A healthy dose of this attitude will serve any writer well.

Once, on my way home from an evening class, I passed a freeway sign that said, "Night Construction." I understood that it meant I should be careful after dark because the construction crews would be taking advantage of the lighter traffic to work on the road. But I also noticed the darkness that seemed to grow from the ground up through the framework of a new bridge as the sunset faded, and I stored away the pleasure I felt in thinking of the road crews "building" night at the end of each day for use in my writing. Comedians and other observers of contemporary life, such as George Carlin or Jerry Seinfeld or Andy Rooney, have built whole careers on noticing and pointing out such anomalies in the way we use language. What is surprising is that so few of us have observed how often and how easily we become accustomed to channeling our perceptions, forgetting to notice. A good writer is a good observer, a person who questions and takes a closer look.

Once the writer has decided to present concrete details and has thought carefully about selecting the telling ones, he still has to consider how to present them, as well as which ones to present. If the writer decides to present the details from the viewpoint of a character directly involved in his subject, it will affect his selection of which details to reveal. Suppose, for the moment, our writer is writing from his own viewpoint, in first person. His manner of expressing details, as well as his choice of details, will reveal his character. *How* people do or say things may reveal more than what they do or say. This is true in some degree of any kind of writing. Even the writer who is preparing a set of instructions on the proper installation of a car radio characterizes himself. The writer decides how detailed the instructions will be. He will choose a tone appropriate to the level of understanding he thinks most of his readers will have in coming to his instructions. He will choose to be prescriptive only or to insert an element of fun in his instructions. The reader will get an impression of the writer's attitude towards his reader and his subject, though it may be perceived as a fairly "standard" one. The reader will form an attitude towards the writer; a positive, even grateful, one if the instructions are clear and useful, and a negative, even angry, one if they are confusing, unnecessarily lengthy, or reveal a superior or careless attitude. The writer cannot completely erase himself from the picture no matter how "objective" the writer may try to be. A completely objective, toneless piece of writing, if it were possible, would still reveal a robot-like non-human writer at the controls. We would probably find it difficult to pay attention.

76

How people say and do things is especially important in describing people in writing. It may be more useful to an essay on the influence of a famous politician to reveal the unique quirks of the politician's speech and the politician's odd habits of gesturing than to quote what the politician said. You may remember your Aunt Gracie gardening not because she had a green thumb, but because she always pulled at her checkered dress and scolded herself when she was doing it. Just as a reader learns a writer's character and attitudes from his viewpoint and style of writing, so can a reader be given clues and dimension by the attitude and manner of speech of specific people included in any piece of writing.

Yet it may prove more difficult to be specific with details than it might at first seem. If I use the word "tree" to describe the tall green plant outside the window, I have used a concrete word with many dimensions. It has both denotative (dictionary definition) and connotative (common associations and relationships many readers are likely to have for the word) meanings. But I could be more specific by calling it a "pine tree" or even more specific by calling it a "Western Yellow Pine." I could also be more specific by describing its relationship to the fence it stands beside, the ground it grows from, or the roof on the house I am viewing it from which does not quite touch it but allows squirrels to easily leap to it from the rain gutter. I may describe it, in other words, in relation to other details. Or I may compare it to other "Western Yellow Pine" trees by detailing its uniqueness (it has a distinctive curve and bare spot on the south side which I have never seen repeated in any other tree) or by direct comparison to something even more visually or sensually evocative (it looks like an old man, balding and hunched over, trying to climb the fence). If I make the comparison by using a word such as "like" or "as," I have created a simile. If I simply say it is "an old man, balding and hunched over, trying to climb the fence," yet the reader knows I am writing about the tree, I have created a metaphor. Repeated use of the same comparisons (metaphors and similes) using different words and details can create a larger sense of comparison called symbol. Symbols can be very effective in essays, just as they are in fiction or poetry. When symbols are repeated over time by many different writers, a level of meaning arises from this commonly accepted and widely repeated metaphorical understanding called myth. A single writer cannot create a myth until it is repeated and reused by other writers, but a single writer can use the existing myths of our culture to expand the impact and meaning of his essay. Be careful to be a little selective in using myths in your essays. It's useful to challenge your reader a time or two, but to load your essay with references to many myths may frustrate and exclude any readers who aren't already familiar with the myths.

The writer may also decide to organize descriptive detail with a pattern, perhaps in relation to the viewpoint, such as the tree as it would look walking past it, from the roof, or from a squirrel's viewpoint. The perspective the writer uses will help determine the meaning of the detail. The most common organizational patterns in description include time (a sequence of events, before/after, etc.), spatial (top to bottom, side to side, etc.) and thematic (developing the detail's multiple meanings through repeated use and reference).

A good writer will also be sure to consider opposites. Sometimes the clearest picture of an object or detail is developed by revealing what it is missing or what it is not. Silence, for example, might be used effectively as a detail by creating a lot of noise and then suddenly removing it. You may need to describe an unfamiliar detail in relation to a more familiar one to make the unfamiliar one clear. You may want to point out an unexpected similarity between details to give a clearer picture. And don't forget humor. It may be

78

effective to exaggerate a detail so much it becomes funny in order to make it revealing. Don't forget that your first and most important purpose is to get and keep the reader's attention.

Narrative

Telling stories is essential to human existence. It's built so deeply into us that many examples of it pass through our daily lives with little notice. Others we try to remember in order to repeat them later. We may try to repeat them faithfully and factually, or we may change and embellish them. In writing, the "story" must have a recognizable point or purpose which the story demonstrates before it can be considered an essay rather than fiction. The significance of the story should be made apparent. The story, then, is really an example of something which has been made clear in the telling or with comment upon the story's example.

Viewpoint is very important to narration because the meaning of any event is determined, in part, by the speaker's angle of view, attitude, and distance from the scene. And since any event that can be narrated must involve a time sequence, the organization of the sequence is especially important. Of course, a narrative may be written chronologically, in the order in which it happened, but this is not always the most effective sequence, and it may also be much more difficult than it appears. Transitions between the scenes become important. A common weakness is to use a time word such as "then" as transition to such an excess that it becomes predictable and therefore boring. You will have to decide how much emphasis and time to give to each of the sequence's various parts and what to leave out. It is literally impossible to tell everything, and it certainly wouldn't be desirable even if it were possible. Meaning is created by selectivity. Equal treatment of all details in a scene would be almost endless and exceedingly boring.

A sequence of events may also be organized in a reverse time sequence, with the concluding event first. Flashbacks may be inserted to shed a different light on the current sequence of events. Events may be orga-

80

nized by a scheme of relative importance that builds or even deliberately deflates a main point. The viewpoint may also suggest an organization of events in much the same way that sense details are organized in a descriptive passage. The viewpoint may move gradually into or through a sequence. It may hover above or watch from the sidelines. The sequence may be reported first hand, through an intermediary, or as if not a person, but an object, such as a camera, had witnessed it. A viewpoint may also change, or alternate, with a second, third, fourth, etc. viewpoint to create perspective. Dialogue may be included with or without comment.

All of the elements contribute to the final effect of an essay and their uses should be determined by the purpose or point of the essay. Whichever elements are chosen, they should, in a narrative, re-create the important moments in a sequence of events. Try to create the experience of the event first, then, if you must, comment on its meaning. Try to make the action immediate and clear. Make things happen in the writing. Don't just sum it up for the reader. Draw the reader into the events.

Carefully constructed events have the power to lead the reader towards the writer's goal. The writer's handling of narrative should point the reader where the writer wants the reader's thoughts to go, but it should not push too hard. Nobody likes a pushy person, unless he or she is an endlessly inventive genius that can keep us entertained even when we don't otherwise much like the overly aggressive behavior. The writer is rarely in the position of being able to assume he or is doing this. A pushy stance must constantly be evaluated to see if it is remaining engaging. A writer needs to take risks to reach the more difficult and effective capabilities of writing, but this must be done selectively and may need the support of additional devices, such as suspense or humor, to affect the reader positively. All of the writer's choices are most likely to result in useful effects when they can be seen as related, and the writer's point, in an essay, is the center of that relationship.

In a narrative approach, the writer must first establish a useful relationship to a sequence of events and then draw one or more conclusions. If the conclusion is clearly implied by the narration, so much the better. The words will have served two functions and that is effective writing. Stating the conclusion may, however, be necessary to clarify the point and assure the reader's understanding of the purpose of the narrative. The reader needs to understand (and feel the experience of) the events as deeply as possible, however, before anybody's opinion will matter.

Example

Often, when you make a statement or wish to demonstrate a point in writing, you will need to back it up with an example. Examples are used to support and clarify general statements or abstract concepts. They can also make the importance of a statement more personally affecting or more widely applicable. Examples are specific instances that show an idea in concrete, specific terms, making it easier for a reader to respond. They explain with clear instances what a group, type, idea, etc. is like.

As with the other methods, the writer's application of examples will depend on the purpose of the writing. Examples may be multiple to suggest the range of the topic, or they may be single cases more fully developed to suggest the depth and impact. An example which tells a small story (narrative) is called an anecdote. Often several of these are used to support a point, but an entire essay could even be a single example if the point it represents is clear in the telling of the example.

As with details in description and sequence in narrative, the order and number of examples must be considered. Effective use of description (and possibly narrative) will be necessary to develop the examples and the points and ideas they represent. The writer must consider the selection of examples carefully. Are they relevant and representative or could they be seen as exceptions?

There are four major types of examples that should be given special consideration when examples are needed.

1. a "typical" case or instance
2. a personal example
3. the experiences of other people
4. statistics

A "typical" example must be not only relevant, clear and sufficiently detailed, it must also be representative. A personal example can make the meaning more direct and provide additional purpose for the essay, though the writer must be careful not to suggest unreasonable bias in the viewpoint as a result of his own experience. It is often easier to write effectively about and "testify" to that which has been experienced first hand. Similar advantages in a less detailed, but apparently more objective, way may result from quoting or pointing to other people as examples. And the sheer weight and suggestiveness of carefully presented numbers may make statistics useful. We all know statistics can be manipulated, but they still retain a strong appearance of authority and objectivity when carefully presented. Often it is a combination of two or three of these types that will provide the best support.

Comparison and Contrast

Comparing and contrasting elements of detail can help make a description clearer. On a larger scale, it can also be a pattern of organization for a complete essay. It can be the writer's way of explaining or analyzing by placing objects or ideas next to each other to provide a clearer and often more affecting understanding. The basis of comparison and the reason for the comparison must be evident for this method to work well, although it may not be necessary to be "equal" or even "fair." A carefully developed humorous exaggeration may make its point as well as a balanced serious presentation. Remember that a characterization of the writer will be drawn by the reader from the approach and style. Would your humorous approach be appropriate for the purpose of your essay? Will it develop a view of its author as a wit or someone who can't take anything seriously? Although the balance of elements in your comparison can be deliberately skewed, it should do so in order to serve the purpose of your essay.

There are two primary patterns for organizing a comparison and contrast essay. Although there are no limits on the number of items which can be compared and contrasted using these patterns, I'll simplify, using only two items to more clearly explain how the two most common patterns are likely to work.

When using the "block" method, the writer considers all that seems of importance to item A first, then does the same for item B, then draws a conclusion. This method has the advantage of fewer transitions and a clearer picture of each item in its total dimensions. It also has the difficulty of the need to effectively leap a larger transitional bridge when the conclusion is drawn because it must effectively link items in each block. Item A may be receding a bit in the reader's memory by the time item B's block is completed and the transition to the conclusion may be correspondingly more difficult.

When using the "alternating" method, the writer moves back and forth between item A and item B, considering the major areas of comparison one by one. This method has the advantage of creating a pattern of movement back and forth as it goes and thus it may not seem as large a leap to the conclusion when it is time to end. It has the difficulty of the need for many more transitions as the pattern of comparisons is set up.

I have used A and B for purposes of clarity in explaining alternatives only. There is no limit to the number of items that can be compared and contrasted, as long as the point of the essay emerges from the details of the development and the writer is able to keep the reader on track.

Don't forget that good description, examples, and perhaps even some narrative may be needed to accomplish a good comparison and contrast. Don't get so tied up in organization using this method that you forget to maintain interest with a good balance of the other elements of writing. When you feel your work getting dull or predictable, fall back on good description and an engaging style.

The rhetorical modes can be thought of as the skeletons of essays. They help provide a strong support system. But don't forget the skin. All form and no content creates well-organized and boring writing that few readers will finish reading.

Analogy

If comparison alone, without contrast, is used in a special way, an analogy results. An analogy is useful when a complicated subject may need comparison to a simpler subject in order to explain it. An analogy can be thought of as an extended metaphor. It takes one thing and compares it to another using only the similarities. If A is the subject, and B is the analogy, A is complicated and the writer is discussing B only in order to explain A. If B becomes part of the subject, the writer has moved from Analogy into Comparison and Contrast. An analogy is weakly chosen when the differences between the subject and the analogy are too intrusive. Analogies are selected for their similarities. If there aren't enough similarities, it isn't a good analogy, and it won't help the writer explain the more complicated subject. If the subject is not difficult to understand, there will be no apparent reason for the analogy.

Sometimes, creating analogies will point out that an apparently simple subject was really much more complex than we might have realized. Analogies, therefore, can also be of use when writing about seemingly ordinary subjects. Of course, an analogy may be created to make a single point in passing on the way to other purposes, but as an organizational device for an essay, multiple similarities between the subject and the analogy will be needed. It is also possible, though difficult, to make several analogies and then link them through a conclusion that shows how they are related.

Since analogies compare only similarities and ignore differences, they create, in argument, what are known as logical fallacies. Keep in mind, however, that, although in the strictest sense analogies are not "logical," they can be imaginative, clear and very effectively persuasive. An analogy is only as good as the writer's ability to express with clarity and effectiveness the analogy's similarities to the subject, so spend time considering several possible comparisons and select your analogy carefully before investing your time and energy in developing it in the writing. A thoughtlessly chosen analogy will only get worse as the writer continues to work with it. A well chosen analogy may gain power from further and deeper exploration of its possibilities. An analogy which appears to be unrelated, yet turns out, thanks to the writer's insight and thoughtful development, to actually reveal important similarities can have a special power, aided by the element of surprise. Good analogies don't usually emerge from ponderous labor, however, but from a willingness to explore and search for the unexpected.

A generous dose of the poet's willingness to look for surprising relationships will be invaluable in uncovering good analogies.

Division and Classification

Often it will be necessary to break something into parts to even begin to write about it. How you choose the categories you will use is very important with this approach. It should be evident to the reader why you chose the categories you did and not others. Your categories should be useful, not arbitrary, and supportive of the purpose of the writing. Your categories should also be complete as a system of sorting information or types, which means you may need a kind of "miscellaneous" category to complete your system by covering anything you may have overlooked. It may help, however, to name it something more appropriate to your subject than merely "miscellaneous." You may even wish to offer some analysis and discussion of possible categorizing methods and mention both the usefulness and the limitations of your choices. This helps convince the reader that you have been thoughtful in selecting the pattern you have chosen. Will you be "objective" or offer a specific, more subjective, viewpoint related to your purpose? How can the other elements of your writing support this choice?

And once you have divided your subject into its parts, does what you learned doing it suggest an even better organization? It may be necessary to put it back together in a new way, to outline a new structure for the essay from the pieces you have created, to reclassify the divided parts.

Division and Classification can be used separately but are really very similar, like mirror images, and can be combined in many ways, including the "block" and "alternating" approaches covered under "Comparison and Contrast." Division is the taking apart of something usually seen as a whole while Classification is the sorting and grouping of scattered items. Classification is usually used when the items appear to be unorganized or organized in a less useful way. Both methods share the idea of forming categories to help organize what you have to say. It may be helpful to outline your categories to see where they may lead you as you go and to juggle and arrange this outline several times as you develop the essay.

A possible sequence to use in developing categories might include:

1. Form your initial groupings.
2. Complete the categories (your system) by considering what you may have left out, including some kind of a "miscellaneous" category in case the reader could discover items that don't fit any of your other groupings.
3. Organize the categories and state the point.
4. Reevaluate and analyze considering:
    1. Why these categories?
    2. Why this way of categorizing?
    3. Will the point be made clear by this approach?
5. Develop an effective introduction.
6. Write the conclusion based on, but further developing and/or applying, the point.

Remember that all of the rhetorical patterns or "modes" are nothing more than patterns of thinking which you probably already use. Writing more effectively with them is simply standing back to take a careful look at how you have been applying them. If you explore carefully the possibilities you may have overlooked, new opportunities will not only be discovered but will begin to be a natural and eventually intuitive part of your thinking. If you take the time to work your way through the application of the pattern slowly and with self reflection and questioning, you will use a wider variety of techniques naturally as you continue writing. What may take days of struggle at first will soon be happening quickly and naturally. The best part is that you won't need to wait for inspiration. You will have learned to create it.

Cause and Effect

The cause and effect method is closely related to our understanding of plot. In fiction, plot is the sequence of events in the story, and if there is a relationship of one event leading to or "causing" another, the plot not only moves the story forward but builds a sense of "rising action" through the increasing links between the events. This same sense of relationship, and often tension, can be created linking ideas instead of events.

A cause and effect approach emphasizes why. Your search will be for relationships and reasons. You may need to conduct your search in stages. What are the immediate causes and/or effects and then what implications do they lead to? They may lead to a surprisingly long or complex series of causes and effects. This is called a causal chain. A causal chain is developed by continually asking why, time after time, until the reason has been taken back to its source. Often, a fully developed causal chain will lead eventually to a silly conclusion, but it may be necessary to reach this silly conclusion in order to know that you have taken the causal chain far enough. When it becomes silly, you backtrack a few steps and there is the useful portion of the chain.

For example, Joe was late for class today because he overslept because he worked too late in order to earn money to buy a flashy new car to impress his girlfriend because he has studied human and animal behavior and believes the male of the species should have the most colorful appearance in order to impress the female of the species who is often colored drably to help protect the young from discovery due to the drab coloring of most ground cover such as weeds and dry grasses in most geographical areas where these species raise their young; therefore, Joe was late for class today because most ground cover is brown. Obviously there is a lapse in logic going on in the development of this causal chain, but it is not unusual to find that after some degree of thoughtful development of a causal chain, it will lapse into illogical reasoning. This is likely to tell you that you have developed the chain far enough to have made important discoveries about how causes and effects for your subject are related. When you have taken it too far, you will know you have taken it far enough.

In our example, we seem to have discovered that Joe was really late because he may be more concerned about impressing his girlfriend than he is about class and might wish to justify this by using an example from his class reading to assuage his guilt over what he may have missed. It is certainly better to have developed the chain too far and backtracked than to discover that you missed some important cause or effect by not going far enough. The causal chain is developed in this manner by linear thinking, as one link of a chain connects to one other link of a chain.

You may also find that, for your subject, you need to consider lateral thinking. It may be that multiple causes or multiple effects are of more importance to your subject than a series of causes leading to distant sources. Consider both possibilities and let the nature of your subject suggest which approach will help lead you to your point. And don't forget that you can choose to use them both.

It is rare, but possible, to have causes considered with very little consideration of effects or vice versa. Usually there will be more than one cause and more than one effect. If not, you may need to make it clear that you have considered this carefully and only after much thought realized that neither multiple causes and/ or effects nor a causal chain exist for your subject.

An outline may be particularly useful when the relationships get complex. It is quite possible that every method mentioned so far will contribute to an effective cause and effect essay. Remind yourself that although it is helpful to consider thinking patterns in isolation to see more clearly how they work, they are usually found in combination in effective writing.

As you develop your cause and effect essay, be sure you don't overlook the obvious first question. The significance of the initial situation must become clear. Otherwise, no one will care what the causes and effects are.

Process Analysis

The simplest way to begin process analysis is to think of it as the answer to the question, "How?" But a few other questions will also have to be answered to write effectively using this method. You must make it clear why the process needs explanation, and you must deal with any misconceptions your reader may be likely to have about the process or any of its steps. The significance of the process must be clear as well as why it is done this way. Each step's importance should be clear, yet not overexplained. It can be easy to fall into a pattern of explaining the obvious with this method, a frustrating waste of time for the reader, unless you're deliberately developing humor. You must avoid boredom and plodding methodical descriptions of obvious steps.

You will probably need division and/or classification as you organize your approach as well as description, narration, cause and effect, and perhaps example or comparison and contrast. Since the writer is not just plugging pegs into holes but creating the holes in the first place, it should be kept in mind that there is no excuse for letting the organization take over what is said. The organization is not a template to be placed over the material. It is your own sense of order and sequence and you can vary it in any way that serves your point. Because the next step is next in the sequence does not mean that you have to explain it in the same way or to the same degree (especially if it might be somewhat clear already) as the previous step. Plodding relentlessly through a sequence of events is not what process analysis is about. It is about consideration of the process and alternatives to the process. The method is used to understand how a process works by taking it apart. And we take it apart to see if there is any better way to put it together.

Narrative employs a sequence (though it need not be chronological), but process analysis considers why that sequence is the one that is used and how it works. Keep your purpose clear and let the methods contribute to it. Don't let the servants become master. When process analysis is the right method for your purpose, you will need to explain how and why something happens, not just what happens next.

Yes, there is a lot to consider using this thinking pattern, but we do it naturally, every day of our lives. We are complex creatures with complex purposes and we require complex means of explaining what we do with our lives. But we have had a great deal of practice doing it, even before we begin to write. Writing with process analysis is simply slowing down and taking a closer look at what we do every time we tell someone how something is done and take the time to explain why it's done that way as we do it.

Definition

Definition as a method in writing is, more accurately, extended definition. This means not just repeating what the dictionary says. It is a means of handling abstract, controversial, complex, misunderstood or otherwise incomplete subjects. It is a larger, alternative, or more deeply considered, picture which presents a new understanding. It can reveal an unexpected angle, perhaps a unique alternative definition. It can redefine and suggest what some word or idea *ought* to mean. It is usually a mixture of several approaches presenting a cumulative view of the idea at hand. It can also be your own specific application, a definition of something you won't find in any dictionary.

The cumulative effect of using several different methods can be powerful with this approach. The writer should consider individually what each of the previous methods covered could do to help with the extended definition. Imagine each touch of a new method as the stroke of a sculptor's mallet as he gradually reveals the underlying figure. Here are a few additional possibilities that may add to the overall effect:

synonyms
antonyms (some subjects can be made clearer
    by presenting their opposites)
characteristics
relationships to a group of similar ideas
the function or use (the idea in action)
elimination (what doesn't it mean)
its source
its history (how has it changed over time)
context (where can or should you find it applied)
speculation (if you imagine a situation, how does
    the subject function in it)

Definition is seldom a strictly factual or provable approach. It is an attempt to create further or varied understanding of something through increasing clarity about its dimensions, applications, importance and interest. A good definition essay reveals, usually by an accumulation of multiple methods and approaches, a new or more complete and deeper meaning. It is often more concerned with complex or unexpected thinking about an idea than it is with having the last word.

When a character in fiction is seen from more than one perspective, the character is said to be "rounded." This is what happens to important characters whose lives we see changing and developing, in contrast to "flat" characters whose purpose in the story is really only to help us see the "rounded" characters with more understanding. An idea presented using only its limited, dictionary definition could be considered as if it were a flat character while the purpose of definition is to create a rounded one. Let us see your definition in a variety of situations and perspectives. You may even wish to let us watch it changing as you develop it. Make your definition come alive.

Argument and Persuasion

The methods covered so far are used most often to inform, to increase understanding. The purpose doesn't have to be to create agreement. But when your writing moves towards wanting to sway the opinions of readers, there are many additional considerations. You can study debate or logic if you wish to cover this in detail, but the writer who is mixing purposes, writing both to inform and to persuade, needs to be especially aware of a couple of major concerns.

The organization of an argument is important. A general structure for an essay can be either statement followed by support or support leading to statement. However, in argument, it is especially important to provide fully detailed support and not to invite your reader to stop with initial statements that seem to demand agreement. Save controversial conclusions until the end of the essay, after you have coaxed and informed your reader about the reasoning used to arrive at them.

It is also a good idea to anticipate the responses of readers who may begin with disagreement. A good strategy is to thoughtfully and carefully consider opposing arguments first, before turning to your own opinion.

It is especially important with this method to be able to distinguish between opinion and fact. You may use both, but presenting an opinion as a fact will quickly weaken your essay.

Consider also your real purpose. Some essays may appear to be argumentative when they are really attempting to shock the reader into recognitions and understandings, not agreements. An outrageous argument may maintain the reader's interest and inform him, even if it does not persuade him to agree. This may not be enough in a courtroom, but it is enough in an essay.

Mixed Methods

By now, you will have seen that it can be difficult to isolate any single approach because most of the best writing mixes the methods and patterns of organizing an essay. While it is useful to look at each one separately, you will soon want to mix their applications. You have considered essays emphasizing specific methods, but the possibilities of mixing methods for dealing with complex subjects and thought patterns are virtually unlimited. Basic organizational patterns and the importance of the three parts of an essay must be understood, however, before one can hope for consistent success in attempting complicated mixtures of methods. Though some may come relatively naturally to you, each of us tends to rely on a select few that have served us well already and the best writers are always trying to expand their repertoire of patterns and effects. In talking with other writers you may discover as well that the patterns and effects that seem natural and more effortless to you are not necessarily the ones that seem that way to them. This is, of course, fortunate for all of us, or we would get bored with all the writers writing in the same way. Yet while we should honor our differences, we should also learn from the methods of others. The best writers have the largest arsenal of available effects and they have used them enough to make them easily available without too much awkwardness. They can achieve this only through practice and the thoughtful, questioning reading of other writers.

As you focus on mixing methods, remind yourself of your discoveries about how transitions are created to help the reader move from one part of an essay to another. This becomes a major area of emphasis and importance when creating more complex organizations. The more complicated our structures and thought patterns become, the more likely it is that we will need a

99

greater ability in handling transitions. The reader is really a very sophisticated thinker when it comes to following transitions. In the modern world, your reader is usually someone who has been exposed to incredible amounts of sophisticated persuasion through movies, commercials, sales pitches, teaching of all kinds, personal and business situations and nearly endless and extremely varied sensory input. This means that thoughtfully handled complex structures are not terribly unusual or difficult for most readers to follow, though it might sometimes appear so to a writer considering applying them. Readers may be suspicious of your motives and their screening behaviors may tune you out if you don't pay enough attention to engaging their interest rather than just expressing your ideas, but if they keep reading, they are capable of following incredibly complex patterns when the writer has provided effective transitions.

Several transitions were covered in Section II, but mixing complex patterns may require even more transitional ability. As your understanding of transitions grows, you will also understand more easily how any recognizable pattern will also provide clues to transitions. If paragraph 1 is a mother speaking, followed by a transitional space, and paragraph 2 is a father speaking, followed by a transitional space, and paragraph 3 is the mother in paragraph 1 speaking again, followed by a transitional space, the reader will assume paragraph 4 is the father in paragraph 2 speaking again unless the reader is told otherwise, even if what is said seems to have no obvious relationship to paragraph 2. These patterns of suggestion can be extremely complicated without losing your reader. You must be careful to see that your reader does not miss your clues, but do not overexplain what you have done.

Above all, trust your impulses. Don't worry about not making sense until long after you've captured the impulse on paper. And never throw any writing away. Put it aside if you haven't yet reached a point in your critical abilities to solve its problems, but trust that you will someday have that ability. Much that I once considered bad in my writing eventually revealed itself to be simply suffering from problems I didn't yet fully understand that were finally not too difficult to solve. Often the problem was inadequate experience with handling mixed methods, experience every writer should strive to continually acquire.

IV. Beyond the Rules

Journals and Notebooks

Nonfiction has traditionally been more associated with journalism than with creative writing, but that has been changing. One of the reasons is the disappearance (or transformation to nonfiction "article" publishing) of many of the magazines that once published fiction for the general reading public. As fiction writers were faced with decreasing possibilities of publication for their work, they turned more frequently to writing nonfiction and they brought their fictional strategies and techniques with them. As the competition for the new nonfiction readership increased, the limitations on how nonfiction writing was perceived began to change as well. Short fiction may not have benefited from this metamorphosis, but nonfiction prospered, and a new and wider range of possibilities for its structures and forms as well as its content was opened.

Now it is often the case that an essay writer will "speculate" on a subject and approach of his or her own interest and attempt to get a magazine or book publisher interested after much of the work is already done. This used to be a much rarer occurrence, with writers proposing articles to magazines and hoping to get hired to write them based on their track record or special expertise. Regardless of the historical perspective, it is clear that a new era of greater latitude and wider interest has emerged in nonfiction writing. "Creative nonfiction" has become a course of study in numerous graduate schools and the boundary between fiction and nonfiction is obscured and often crossed for creative effect.

It has always been a good idea for any writer to keep a journal or notebook, but it has become an even more useful possibility for nonfiction writers than it used to be because of this wider range of possibilities. A nonfiction writer can collect fragments, random thoughts, momentary speculations, apparently insignificant pieces of unrelated phrases and observations, even descriptions of the weather or diary entries, knowing that the potential for their use in essays is very great indeed.

This also frees the writer of essays to construct essays as many poets write poems, from curious juxtapositions of elements composed at different times in different places about different subjects, a technique once thought of as only for the experimental writer. With this approach an essay writer can more easily build an essay piece by piece rather than write one in a more traditionally linear fashion. And essay writers are now freed as well from the traditional constraints of complete sentences, full paragraphs, repetitive coherence. Using a notebook can help you recognize the power and suggestive possibilities of fragments, lists, even simply an unusual word that you might desire an excuse to use. Notebooks make it easier to focus on variations in sequencing and the creation of transitions. They allow surprise and the excitement of discovery to occur while assembling completely separate moments of perception which can then lead to further perceptions. The writing can be more easily generated even when the author is no longer in proximity to the subject.

Working in this way is also a very good opportunity to discover the themes and "obsessions" (a positive rather than negative characteristic for a writer) that exist even in apparently very different moments of writing. All great writers have developed their particular recurring themes over the course of their careers. The good ones return to them with something to add each time and the sequence of their work becomes a larger "progress" as fascinating to watch as any of the author's individual works.

Of course this also means that you'll never have to start from scratch again. Unless you want to. Writer's block will be replaced by "What do I work on first?"

Writing for Life

While most of us wouldn't have any trouble acknowledging that we are constantly practicing the arts of speaking and thinking, we often don't recognize that writing is as basic as either of them. We often forget that writing letters, making lists, filling in forms, and endless daily tasks we might think of as relatively insignificant engage us with words as written communication on such a regular basis that we should be recognizing the "written thought" that enters our lives relentlessly. If we realized that the relationship of writing to words is not just recording on paper but the entire process of creating and shaping ideas, we might begin to see that writing the words down is only the last act in a sequence of absolutely essential life skills. Even to those who can neither read nor write, the process of writing is at work in the very ability to shape words into sentences. And if we were to acknowledge this, we might also recognize that both speaking and thinking are affected and even shaped by the relationship we establish to written expression, even when it reaches us indirectly.

Writing is such a basic cornerstone of a life's growth that we should no more think of neglecting it than we would think of not thinking or speaking. Yet too many still see it as a skill needed only in special circumstances. E. M. Forster said, "I never know when I'm not writing." Perhaps we should see its meaning as, "I never know when I'm not living."

Find Your Own Structures of Meaning

The methods of organizing thought presented here are the most frequently applied and the possibilities of new applications of them will never be exhausted. Even so, good writers are always searching for ways of doing it differently, not just out of rebellion but because they know language and its uses, like the ideas contained in it and their applications, are constantly changing. Percy Shelley called poets the "unacknowledged legislators of the world." Language is so basic to expressing ideas that when you change or add to the ways we can use it, you change the very ideas it expresses. Language use is a constant search for meaning. Every writer participates in this search because every writer holds the possibility of using his differences and discoveries in a unique way. While every writing teacher will tell you there are quite a number of things they see over and over in the writing of beginners, they will usually also acknowledge that even beginners sometimes create new and effective ways to say it that even a professional would envy. Read voraciously to increase your variety of tools, but don't forget you already have the most important one. You have your individual and inimitable combination of behavior, thought and language use, your personality. Much of writing isn't a search for a way to be different but a search for how to create a context in which the difference you already possess can be seen for its real value.

Not About Life but Life Itself

When an essay writer sits down to write about a subject, the attitude he brings to the job determines a great deal about the degree of success to be achieved. Try thinking of your writing not as "about" something but as the thing itself. Not "about" a life, but the living creature.

When you write, you are creating a new life. Get inside it and live there. Even when it is your own life you are writing about, you must re-experience it fully to be able to give it to the reader. Don't just stand back and talk about it. Move in and move around in its skin. Create the life. Don't just summarize it. Show us what it feels like by doing it. Don't just tell us what it meant.

"Show us; don't tell us," is the most common advice given to any writer, but the ways in which we tend to tell rather than show are voluminous. Starting with a constructive "from the inside out" attitude towards what you are doing when you write will go a long way towards shifting the focus. Write a life instead of a description of a life.

Action, Not Just Reaction

A common problem for poets that often can be seen in essay writers is the natural human impulse to concentrate on the meaning of the events rather than the events themselves. Of course we want to make meaning out of our experience, but in writing we can forget that the reader hasn't had our experience. We must relive it for them before they can respond with the same reactions that we will. So focus on the events that cause the meaning, not just the meaning. The secret is that the writer can not be totally objective in trying to recreate the cause of meaning and the meaning will often be expressed indirectly, and more effectively, through the author's style, tone, techniques, choices of effects, diction, syntax and a hundred other more subtlely persuasive possibilities than simply telling the reader what the experience means. In this way the words are performing two functions at once and writing which is doing more than one thing at a time is always more powerful. There are few experiences more convincing for a reader than having been persuaded towards an understanding without even knowing how it happened.

Stranger than Fiction

One of the difficulties encountered by essay writers has to do with the *appearance* of reality, something which is not always the same as reality itself. In writing nonfiction you must sometimes deal with a situation in which you are writing about something that actually happened and yet it contains elements that seem unbelievable. It might appear to be the case that simply writing it down carefully should be enough, but writers must also deal with the impressions and expectations that writing creates for the reader. Writing nonfiction sets up the expectation that if you are making something up, you will reveal this and not just pretend that it's true. The flip side of this expectation occurs when you are writing something which is true but appears to be made up. You must deal with the *appearance* of a lie because your real goal is not simply to tell the truth but to tell it in a way that can be received usefully by the reader.

In fiction, if the reader has a reaction that separates him from the story, the writer can draw the reader back in by having a character, or the narrator, acknowledge a similar reaction. This way the reader's difficulty becomes part of the story and the reader is again participating in it.

In nonfiction, the appearance of a lie (or a "fiction") operates in much the same way. Acknowledge that it might appear unbelievable but actually happened. Take a moment or two to deal with your own incredulity at how truth can be stranger than fiction. Then, when you move on, you will have the reader sharing your reaction to the truth instead of questioning your integrity.

Presentation

If it's not already apparent, take some time to think about how thin the line between fiction and nonfiction really is. What is the truth and what is made up? Isn't the "truth" at least partially made up the minute a writer interprets its meaning for a reader?

If there is really so little difference between fiction and nonfiction, then why do they usually appear in such identifiably different forms?

The answer is presentation. The tone and attitude contained in the style, the forms and structures used to present the material, the associations to previous writing using similar approaches, even the title, are all part of the expectations the writer creates very quickly in a piece of writing.

The difference between fiction and nonfiction has more to do with the "clues" the writer sets up for the reader to follow than it does with the "truth" of the material itself. Test this by rewriting a piece of fiction as an essay or an essay as a story. What did you have to change tomakethe transition? You will likely be surprised at how easy it is to cross that boundary between them.

Out of Confusion, Boredom, and Excess

I often hear writers complain of writer's block and it makes me embarrassed to admit I haven't suffered from it in such a long time that I simply can't remember what it's like. This has nothing to do with any inherent genius on my part. It's simply a natural result of recognizing that good writing often begins with seemingly unimportant and uninspired moments and ideas. The basic principle of art that motivates much of my writing is the idea that art is not the result of genius or talent, but the perseverance to follow something, even something very ordinary, farther than others have done.

Every piece of writing contains clues to where it might go if only the writer could read them. Workshops and group editing sessions can be a great help in learning to recognize potentials in early drafts of writing. So can the experience of reading a great quantity of unpublished work that being an editor for a while can provide. Teaching writing and the huge quantity of paper grading that comes with it can also do this. However you can gain this experience, if you approach it looking for possibilities to push to a further reach of idea and imagination and learn to analyze how the gears of the writing are being engaged or disengaged as it moves along, then you will have the information you need to extend the work that has already been set in motion. Eventually you will find this process of unearthing possibilities so fascinating that even a technical possibility of sentence structure, a seldom used word, or a strange combination of point of view and style might be enough to spark your interest in seeing how far it might go if you push on it.

The real subject of all writing is your own mind. All you have to do is trust that it will take you somewhere interesting if you let it explore what's really going on with its own impulses. Try not to force direction from a sense of the right way to do it. Don't limit your subjects. If a "rule" interests you, test it. Then try writing in violation of the rule. Think about the help rules can provide *when you're editing* your work, not when you're creating it. Don't be afraid to make up rules of your own. Or to change rules when they are no longer helpful. When "rules" that have been tested really work and prove to be frequently useful, you will not need to worry about writing "correctly." You will simply learn to trust the tools you have used to develop interesting work.

Some of these tools will follow traditional good advice. Some may not. You will need tools of both types to complete your best work.

The Balance Sheet

Much of what is often seen as the "rules" of essay writing is really only a set of guidelines based on what works more often than it doesn't. A more useful way to explore and discover the potential of writing is to think of it as a sequence of related "choices" with advantages and disadvantages to each choice.

When you see something in your writing that isn't working, don't just eliminate or correct it, consider what could happen if you develop it instead. There are always two choices when working with a weakness. Something that appears "wrong" in the work may be wrong only because it appears unthinking or accidental. Try repeating the "mistake" deliberately, adding meaning and direction to the "wrong" moment in your work. It may be "wrong" only because its purpose is not yet clear.

Even if you fail to make the weakness into a strength, you will have learned more about writing from your willingness to explore its potentials. It may surprise you by popping up in a more productive context later in your writing.

Think of your work as a gathering of good and bad moves that changes with each new subject and approach. Change any one of those moves and it sends reverberations out through all the other moves, changing their effects as well. Your job is to find the combination that works best together.

Creative Editing

Writers who have not yet learned to enjoy revising and editing their work are missing much of the real joy of writing. You can bring the same excitement of creation to this work that you have when a new idea hits you. When you realize that a discovery made while editing can open up completely new directions and spawn new writing, a whole new world of interest is created.

Editing is not just tedious touch-up of spelling and punctuation but questioning and discovery about the relationships of subjects and techniques. It is, at its best, radical and exploratory. It should be exciting and fresh, not just a once-over application of a dictionary and an English handbook.

Good editors make better writers. Good writer/editors can produce interesting writing when inspiration-based writers have run dry. Good editors work with the larger, more important questions about what the writing could be if it was nudged left or right or turned on its head. Good editors don't just "correct," they create.

Padding; a Lean Style

It's usually a good idea to overwrite when creating the first draft or when in doubt. But this can become a repetitive bad habit as well if the good editor in you isn't alert enough to notice. Not all subjects and styles are most effective with the greatest possible detail. Some benefit from directness and simplicity. Writers like Ernest Hemingway and Raymond Carver have shown us the profound complexity that can be created with simple language styles. For most of us, this is not something that will come naturally. It requires careful consideration of each word in the same way you might expect a poet to work. But the secret of a strong lean style is not just selecting the right noun and verb and limiting the modifiers placed with them. It is also paying close attention to the small words that we often ignore, words like "the" and "this" and "and" and "when." The writer of a lean style is using the words we tend not to notice very carefully to carry more of the work. He is trying to get the same job done without calling so much attention to how the words are doing it. By paying careful close attention to ordinary words, he is trying to keep the reader focused not on the words but on the subject.

Even if you have no desire to write a lean style, it's extremely helpful to do this kind of editing and thinking for a while to discover how much power and usefulness can be achieved from simple direct statement. All good writing contains contrast. If you're a "lyric" writer, a moment of lean statement provides an important contrast and strengthens both the dominant style and the moment of difference by stretching the range and exaggerating the effects of both styles. And if you're a "minimalist" writer, your lean style appears more direct and powerful by contrast to a moment of lyric beauty.

Overexplanation and Wordiness

Detail. Detail. Detail. Says the writer creating the first draft and rightly so. How can you know where you're going and what you might accomplish getting there if you leave something out along the way? And it's so easy to be too focused on your conclusions and forget to provide the information from which you drew them.

But after that detailed first draft has arrived, it's time to revise and edit and to pay close attention to the habits you most likely have developed of relying on certain words and word combinations that don't really say very much. There are no absolutes, but a good place to start is by marking and paying closer attention to any phrase or sentence patterns that are being repeated. Often a tendency to think and write in certain patterns creates an unneeded use of "filler" words to produce the pattern again when the content doesn't really need this. Often we are somewhat aware of this and create different words to fill the pattern which are really saying the same thing. In editing for this, you are looking for repeated ideas and meanings as well as words. If a word is repeated with new meaning, it is not repetition. If a new word is used that really means the same thing as something already said, it is repetition. You are looking for unnecessary information and repetition of ideas, not just words.

As with other editing tools, don't forget that "wordiness" has its purposes and should not always be edited out. Sarcasm and irony, for example, may require wordiness to accomplish the purpose of creating a desirable negative attitude towards the subject or speaker.

Learn to identify wordiness and question its uses, but don't overlook its potentials. Make your style reflect choices, not accidents.

Relative Quality; Improving the Neighbors

Context is one of the most powerful tools a writer can have at his disposal. A passage of writing that looks poorly done and clumsy can take on incredible power when placed in the right context. The key is to create a sense of deliberate effect and encourage the reader to trust the writer's purpose in doing things which might appear to be unorthodox.

One of the easiest and most powerful ways of changing or creating context is the "frame." Imagine this effect similar to the changes in perception and understanding that can occur when a painting is framed. It can take on a sense of balance and completion that might have been almost absent unframed. It can change the places to which the viewer's attention is drawn and create a new understanding.

In writing, the most common "frame" is a contrast of some kind placed before the body of the work and returned to after it. This gives both a sense of structure and an often useful contrast to the central "development" of the work. This can be done to the work as a whole or to any selected portion of the work. You can also exaggerate the effect by varying other elements of the writing to contrast the frame and the body, such as verb tense, time, style, scene, point of view and so on.

This might seem like a great deal of work, but when it has become clear how context works to create meaning, it can often be done with very few words. Sometimes even the title of the work alone or the use of section titles can create a completely new context for the meaning of the work.

All good writing contains conflict and contrast is an essential means of creating it. Context can create that contrast.

Qualification and Contradiction; Yes and No

In trying to describe something accurately, a writer often finds an increasingly lengthy string of modifiers and descriptive language diluting the sense of certainty that he is trying to create with the detail. This is often not really a result of too much detail, but a result of trying to resolve certain kinds of conflict that might better be encouraged. When something is complex enough to contain both a yes and a no, a black and a white, the writer may move to lengthier and lengthier descriptions of "maybe" or "gray." Try instead to assert a clear yes with great certainty. Then assert equally clearly and with even greater certainty that no is true. Let the contradiction be the "maybe" you were looking for. It's definitely a solid black *and* it's most certainly a pure white, rather than it's a confused gray.

Group Editing

Editing calls for an attempt at objectivity. The writer must stand back from the work and try to see it as a new reader, with no knowledge of how the writer would see it. Being objective about ourselves is perhaps the most difficult thing there is. You can't just decide to do it and achieve it. It takes practice and it takes learning the critic's ways of thinking in order to analyze and discover the less apparent meanings and potentials contained in a piece of writing.

Since it's so much easier to be objective about someone else, why not take advantage of it to try out the questioning and exploration that will be necessary to improve your own work. Try to discover constructive ways of improving your own writing through analyzing and questioning the strengths and weaknesses of the writing of others. You will be helping them improve their work while you are learning the skills to become more objective about your own.

Don't forget that strictly negative criticism overlooks the achievements and potentials that exist in the writing. Strictly positive criticism feels good but doesn't help the work get any better. A balance sheet approach of what's working and what isn't working may help the author to find the combination of choices that will increase the work's effectiveness.

The hidden secret about why group editing is so useful is that it isn't just the discussion of your own work that benefits you, it's the practice learning to analyze and edit and the more objective perspective that this creates that will lead you eventually to a greater ability to use the same tools on your own work.

Some Editing and Revising Questions

1. Have you given serious consideration to drastic change in the organization of your essay? What would happen if you put the last paragraph first? If you reversed the order of your approach?

2. Have you considered writing your essay from another viewpoint? Don't forget to consider the more unusual ones: multiple (we), nonhuman, camera, progressive (moving gradually past, into, out of, etc.). Have you considered creating a mask (a character or "screen," perhaps nonhuman or the opposite sex) to speak through? Could your essay be more effective if spoken by someone (or something) other than you? Or you at another age?

3. Have you considered using more than one viewpoint? Sometimes the contrast of differing viewpoints can best serve your purpose.

4. What is your real subject? Did you make any discoveries while writing? Could there be a hidden subject in your material? In writing about a memory, for example, did you discover anything about why you remember that event instead of some other one. Is there anything which may not be obvious that affected your choice of subject? To some degree, nearly anything you write is about how you perceive the world. Is a part of your real subject hidden in that fact? Give careful and critical consideration to your subject after you've written a draft. Perhaps you needed a bit of freedom to get started writing. Fine. Now find the real subject, the one that carried your interest deeper. If you don't really care much about your subject, it's going to show. You can't expect your reader to work harder to be involved in your subject than you did. Be honest with yourself and your reader. If you tried to write about wanting to buy

a car and having no money and you got angry at not being able to do it or bored with trying to explain something that doesn't seem like it will ever change, then anger, frustration, or boredom may be your real subject, not buying a car.

5. Always treat your unfinished draft like an indestructible enemy. Turn him on his head, put his arm in his bellybutton, put his eyes in the back of his head and you will not harm him. Perhaps you will discover something important by rearranging his parts or looking at him as if he were a different creature entirely. You can always put him back the way he was by returning to an earlier draft.

6. Writing and reading are part of the same act. Have you thought about your reader? What can you discover by thinking about yourself as the reader of your essay?

7. Writing is an act of discovery, of learning. What discoveries did you make about yourself, about the world, about how you bridge the gap between people, between experiences, while you were writing or thinking about writing your essay? Should these discoveries be included as part of your subject?

8. Is there some phrase, image, sentence in your rough draft that stands out? Why? Could it lead you to a more interesting subject or approach? Don't be afraid to let a good moment in your writing carry you a new direction. You may learn more from it than from years of struggle to force your essay into a preconceived mold.

9. How will you start your essay? Have you written an unneeded introduction in warming up to your subject? What happens if you throw out a paragraph or two? Should you start in the middle of a scene or step gradually into it, describing as you go?

10. How much explanation do you really need? Can you show us what you mean instead of telling us about it? Have you given us a chance to see, hear, touch instead of summarizing what you mean? Have you re-lived the experience for your reader or just summed it up?

11. Indifference is deadly. Don't settle for "okay." If you were a comedian and every time you told a joke the audience said, "It's okay," instead of laughing, would you consider yourself successful?

12. Always send your rough drafts to your editor. You are, of course, your own editor (or your editing group is, for now), but when you are the editor, imagine yourself as the harshest, most unaccepting, nitpicking, but honest, direct and experienced creation you can. He should delight in finding anything you could have done better and get a big kick out of discovering how your whole approach was wrong. Give this character a name and description if it helps create a more critical viewpoint. This grumpy perfectionist has got to be sharp. Nothing gets by that could have been done better.

13. How have you ended your essay? Is your package tied up in a neat little bundle that makes everything so clear there's nothing left to think about? Have you overwritten? Could it have been said quicker and more directly? What would happen if you dropped the last sentence? The last paragraph? Point the way if you like, suggest answers, leave clues, but don't write what's already been suggested or take the steam out of your carefully chosen development details by trying to nail it all down with an ending that doesn't give your reader room to think. Use your ending to draw the reader back into the essay. Don't let him throw away your work by summing it up in a conclusion that merely re-

states what you've already said. Make your conclusion add something to your essay while it comes to its point.

14. Does your title serve a useful function? Is it only a slapped-on label that works as well as a dozen others? Try to make your title memorable, suggestive, haunting. Writing is a way of thinking. Use your title to help encourage your reader to think in new and interesting ways, just as you must to interest yourself in the subject. Naming things is one of the great discoveries of childhood. Bring it back with new ways of "naming" in your title as well as in your essay. Is there a phrase that applies to your essay which may have a new meaning after reading the essay? Is there an implication suggested by your essay that you could point to with the title? Does your ending refer back to your introduction? Could your title have a place in this "frame?" Could your title contrast to your essay by expressing an apparent opposite? Can you eliminate any wordy explanation of viewpoint, setting, time, etc. by putting it in the title?

15. Finally, the fine tooth comb: Word by word, are any unnecessary? Can you be more specific, more active, more suggestive? Get out the thesaurus. Are any words or combinations of words ordinary, heard too often? If you have used simple words and sentences, does the approach suit the subject and purpose? If you have used more unusual words, are there places where a switch to something direct and simple would be effective? Can you make something simple stand out by surrounding it with more colorful words or something colorful stand out by surrounding it with simple words? Don't be afraid of using words your reader may not know. Just be sure you've used them clearly. Don't forget to comb the title. Consider every word carefully.

Does it seem like a lot to go through every time you write a short essay? And for every draft? It is, but it gets easier. Go through it thoroughly a few times and you'll gradually find yourself asking and answering these and many other questions naturally as you write and rewrite, and you will begin looking for new ones to learn from. You will find them by reading as a writer reads, by trying to understand how it was done whenever you find something effective. You will have developed a framework for becoming a better and better writer (and editor) as long as you continue to read and write.

Stolen Techniques

Take from one writer and you have plagiarism. Take from a thousand and you may have genius. All writers learn from other writers. It is the filtering of the borrowed knowledge through the complex interwoven web of the writer's personal knowledge and experience that makes it belong to the new writer. The broader that knowledge and experience, the more completely the assimilation is likely to be reflected as an original product of the new writer.

One way to expand one's essay writing abilities is to bring techniques and possibilities to nonfiction that are more commonly learned in other fields. Study fiction to learn how to use plot, how to create better character development, or what to do to create effective uses of point of view and bring that knowledge to your attempts at essay writing. The boundary between different writing genres is much thinner than our labels would suggest. Good essay writing often contains good fiction, despite the label of nonfiction. After all, fiction tells the truth too. It just does it in a different way.

And if you study poetry to discover the possibilities of a very lyrical or condensed style, it will enhance your abilities in creative nonfiction. Poetry is particularly useful in revealing strategies of organization and transition as well as style. The structure of a poem is usually completed much faster than the structure of an essay and a thoughtful consideration of a poem's structure may reveal techniques which are equally useful in nonfiction but often more hidden in the slower development.

You don't have to limit this application of techniques from other fields to just writing. Study film and television to see how imagery and visual shifting of attention (another form of transition) can direct and change the focus for the audience. Go to the theater and study dialogue. Several poets I know have taken structures for poems from discoveries in science. They are so fascinated by what science has to teach us about the world we live in that they are attempting to apply this new knowledge to how they organize and present their creative world, an attempt at a new kind of "organic" structure. I know both poets and fiction writers who study comedians and jazz to learn pacing, how to handle the rhythms and timing of their presentation. Some writers study obscure fields of knowledge and work it into their writing to keep the content fresh and to take advantage of their excitement about learning something few people know. It helps them maintain the enthusiasm of discovery in their writing.

There is an additional benefit from exploring other "worlds" because often the writer can learn something useful and unexpected from placing his subject in a context that is foreign to it. The surprising revelations of a new home for your ideas may expand your understanding of them and create additional interest in them. When in doubt, move. You can always come back if the new location doesn't offer anything helpful. Writers have a great advantage over performing artists. If it doesn't work, they just remove it. A writer doesn't have any risk attached to trying something new. If it fails, no one needs to know. But if it succeeds, the writer gets all the credit.

Implied Meaning

One of the most effective of writing devices is implied meaning. A developing writer will often discover this operating in the work by "accident,"which is actually subconscious "intent," but it may feel like an accident. If he's thoughtful about it, he will begin to push it further, more deliberately. This discovery usually reveals its potential when the writer is learning revision and editing skills because it can sometimes be created by removing unnecessary wordiness during the process of revision. But it can go much farther than just giving the style a more direct, leaner tone.

Try breaking the work into small units, a paragraph or two or even smaller, during revision. Now read portions of the work with a unit or two missing. You may be very attached to the missing unit because of nice phrasing or other style effects, but try to set that aside. Have you really lost much meaning by leaving out the unit? Sometimes it will surprise you to find out that what looked essential to say has actually been suggested clearly by the writing which surrounds it. When you find this to be true, try leaving out two, three or even more units. Do you find you have an urge to say things directly which may already have been implied indirectly? Occasionally it may be useful, but most often, writers, especially essay writers, become overly concerned with explanation. Writers need to be concerned with meaning and understanding, yes, but there are better ways than explanation to achieve them.

Implied meaning, then, can be thought of as an extension of the basic writing principle of, "Show us; don't tell us." The more you can reveal without having to explain it, the stronger the connection to the reader.

Juxtaposition

A technique that helps to create implied meaning is juxtaposition, the placing of one element next to another (without explaining why it's being done). When this works well, the differences between the elements create an implied additional meaning for the work. When the reasons for placing the elements next to each other can be known by implication, it also eliminates unnecessary word transitions, another kind of explaining.

To begin exploring juxtaposition, try cutting up your essay into parts, physically, with scissors. Move the parts around to see what is suggested to the reader by placing surprising sections of the work next to ones which seem, at first, to have little or no logical relationship to each other. What is suggested by this? Remember that if you have written with an interesting style, the reader will assume what you have done is thought out, that it has a purpose behind it. If you assume that this random act is not random, what purpose might there be? Once you have discovered possible uses for this arrangement, you can nudge other elements of the writing to support the new purpose.

As you explore the implied meanings created by this technique, notice that any time a pattern is created by the unexpected placement of units, the pattern adds an additional element of implication. Just as starting a new paragraph for each change of speaker in a dialogue between two people eliminates the need for "he said" and "she said," a pattern in the arrangement of unexplained juxtapositions of units of writing can offer implied explanation.

Many writing techniques, including this one, are a kind of short hand for prose writers, much like the techniques a poet would use to make more meaning with fewer words. These techniques require closer attention on the part of the reader, but they also honor the reader's intelligence. A careful reader will feel rewarded for the attention they are being asked to pay to the work by a more involved relationship to the writing. They will no longer be reading for information only.

Allusions and Epigraphs

Reference to the work of other writers and well-known people can often be made during the writing to add dimension to the meaning of the subject. Be careful that obscure allusions are not losing the reader. This happens when the meaning of the allusion in its original context must be fully understood to follow the train of thought. Effective allusions are more often an enhancement than an essential element of the writing. Their purpose is to help provide context and perspective to what is being said. They are not the thing being said itself, but an additional level of understanding of its context and relationships. Use them freely, but don't rely on them for the central thrust of your development unless they are so widely known that almost no one could miss them. Allusions can help us understand more fully, moments of viewing the landscape that surrounds us as we make our journey.

Epigraphs operate much like allusions, but they are quotes relating to the content of the writing that provide perspective even before the reader begins the main text. They can be used to direct the reader's attention as he begins to read as well as to provide perspective on the subject (see page 16). They are quoted or placed in italics and their source is identified. They appear below the title but before the writing. Epigraphs can also be used to deliberately force the reader to consider something about the subject that might not otherwise appear to be related. Like titles, they can be used to add unexpected interpretations to the meaning of the work.

Satire and Hyperbole

Exaggeration is a powerful device in writing. It can create humor and it can redirect the meaning. If exaggeration is recognized as a consistent device, the meaning begins to change to the reverse of what is literally being said. Sarcasm or irony become apparent. If this device is used over the length of the work, the result is satire, an honored and effective form of discourse.

But reversal of meaning is not the only way to use exaggeration. Sometimes, when it is used momentarily in an essay, it may reveal a surprising truth of a more serious nature. Not all exaggeration leads to humor.

There is no rule that can be used to determine how exaggeration will work, but it might help to remind yourself that there are always two possibilities when dealing with a moment of difference in the writing. You can remove it to enhance the flow and consistency of the work, or you can increase its effect by exaggeration or repetition. Don't forget that when something isn't working as well as you might want it to, it might be because you haven't used the effect enough to make it work.

V. The Writing Life

Living It

When writing has become much more than a servant to occasional requirements, it can enrich and complete the writer's experience of life. In the same way a musician might be capable of a greater appreciation of bird calls or an artist might be better attuned to the delightful surprises of unexpected color, a writer can become a receiver of life in ways that would otherwise be unavailable.

And yet a writer has another advantage too. In addition to becoming more attentive to the wonders of words, every other subject on earth is also directly available to the writer. The writer has only to study thoroughly any subject and it becomes a part of the writer's world of expression. He does not have to play an instrument to appreciate music and create it through words. He does not have to use paint to create an image.

A writer's world is, perhaps, as unlimited as any one could hope to live. It requires only a receptive attitude to the possibilities. It allows you to serve your own higher purposes and to search for your own reasons. Use the work in your own way, for your own growth. Then make it available to the reader.

Compatriots

A writer's work is done mostly alone. And writing is not, in our society, as appreciated as it ought to be, especially when it comes to the difficulties of publishing and making a living. An aspiring writer may have many discouragements and denigrations to endure while developing his craft. It can be a very useful idea to develop a network of like-minded friends and writers, people who appreciate what you are trying to do. I have known many writers who received little or no encouragement from their own families. Writing is often seen as a wasteful way to spend one's life. Writers are often thought of as dreamers, as unrealistic. Well, writers are dreamers because we all are dreamers. Writers merely acknowledge and encourage their natural tendencies and tell the truth about their desires.

The world we live in is competitive and a dedicated writer's first concern is not getting ahead in the external world but developing the work. In the sometimes lonely isolation in which writing is created.

I have seen writers achieve early success for what seems to be a "natural" talent and quickly fade away when it came time to progress in the only way really possible, doing battle with one's own difficulties, alone. And there have been many examples of writers who achieved little or no recognition in their own lifetime, but gave the world a lasting gift of their achievement and led a fuller, if unrecognized, life in doing it. To my way of thinking, that is a life well spent, even if the author dies unaware of the recognition that may yet come of that achievement.

An aspiring writer would do well to counterbalance the negativity he can expect to surround him about his abilities and life choice by surrounding himself as best he can, without interfering in his working time, with people who share an immediate appreciation for the worth of such efforts. They don't have to like ev-

135

erything you write, or even anything you write, but they must live with an implicit understanding of the value of living your life more completely through writing.

Editors

There are famous stories of editors, such as Maxwell Perkins, who did such an extraordinary job of editing the works of now famous writers that the distinction between writing and editing might once have seemed clear. Personally, I doubt this was ever the case, but if it was, it no longer is. The fiscal realities of contemporary publishing have led to fewer and fewer editors who can afford the time to edit as a writer would edit, nudging the work to its full potential. And with the incredible volume of available manuscripts, they don't have to do this. There's another work, already well edited, just waiting to be published. And anyway, why would any author not use every tool possible to help his work be seen as more accomplished?

Editing should not be left to the publisher. If a writer is lucky, a good editor can notice things and raise useful questions about the direction the work is going, but a good writer should not rely on the editor. Only after editing the work himself and using every trick he knows should the writer even allow the editor to see the work.

Many writers are concerned about their work being altered during publication. The choice always remains with the writer. He can withdraw the manuscript and seek publication elsewhere if he does not approve of changes demanded by a publisher. But why leave yourself open for the possibility of confusing and difficult decisions created by possibilities and questions raised by an editor which you have not thought of? Why not complete the editing process as fully as you can? If you do a thorough enough job of it, it is much less likely that any major concerns will arise during the publication process.

One final word of caution. Despite the general trend, there are still some good editors out there. Do not reject suggestions simply because you didn't think of them first. Give each suggestion careful consideration and learn from it if it helps your work. Consider it again as you create new work, but never give it greater authority than your own instincts. Weigh the possibilities carefully, but take responsibility for the end result. The writer always has the final word.

Feed Your Head

No, I'm not having a Jefferson Airplane flash-back. A writer is a bridge for the reader into many possible worlds. It would be foolish to use that bridge only to enter a singular world of writing, no matter how interesting that might be. You can't "get off the subject" if you only have one subject. Part of the enjoyment of the growth that writing provides is finding unexpected relationships between differing subjects. Let your interests carry you to little known, obscure places and trust that the time will come when that seemingly trivial or esoteric bit of knowledge will emerge surprisingly and effectively in your writing. A writer is first of all a curious person, someone who doesn't brush aside information others might see as useless.

Explore. Let your impulses and intuitions carry you where they will. Your real subject when you write is your own mind. Make it an unusual one.

Submission

To submit, is not, to a writer, to give up. It is the natural process of allowing others to see your work who might be able to help it reach a wider audience. Some writers get so involved in this that they neglect the real work, the writing. But recognition is also a writer's aphrodisiac. It can provide useful incentive to give the work an extra level of energy and enthusiasm.

It can be a danger to submit before you're ready, not only because you are more likely to be rejected, but because if you're accepted and the work isn't your best, you will be embarrassed by it later.

But let's assume you're ready. Now you've made it, right? Out popped an essay several readers admire. They think you're brilliant, talented, headed for fame and fortune. Okay, let's admit it. Life is full of rejection and the problem is compounded for a writer because you usually don't really know why your work is being returned. A writer with experience as an editor knows about the numerous reasons entirely separate from quality that play a part in the game of publication. Good writing increases your odds of winning, but good writing is often rejected.

So be prepared for rejection. I like to wait until I have several things ready and submit them at the same time. That way, when I receive a rejection, I still have other work out there being considered. And it seems to make it easier to treat submission as the clerical chore it really is. I don't torture myself over decisions about where to send it. I just keep a file of the magazines I would most like to appear in and work my way down the list. Of course, the better the magazine, the higher the chances of rejection. But it has also been my experience that lesser known magazines reject good work nearly as frequently.

Use common sense when submitting your work. Try to remain aware of your own psychology. Submitting your work raises questions of how you yourself feel about it, not just the editors. Don't submit blindly. Spend some time reading the magazines you're going to consider sending your work to. Inappropriate submission of types of work not published by the magazine are far too common. They waste everyone's time and money. And yes, it does cost money to submit your work, but the magazine should *not* charge a fee to consider it.

Here's the standard. Nicely typed and neatly printed pages with your name and address on the top of the first page. Put the work in an envelope with another envelope inside that has your address and postage on it for return. Now imagine it takes a couple of dozen tries to find the right place for the work. Even if your piece is short enough to need only one stamp, that's 48 stamps and envelopes, to say nothing of your time. This is the cost of submitting your work. Another good reason to be sure your work is the best you can make it before you submit.

Notice I didn't mention cover letters. I have experimented with them several times and found no correlation whatsoever between the rate of acceptance and the inclusion of a cover letter. If the magazine wants your piece, they'll notify you and ask for a contributor's note. That's the time to tell them who you are. Yes, there are magazines that pay closer attention to the work of known writers and if you're one of them, maybe a cover letter helps. But if you really are known, you don't need a letter to show it, and if your focus is really on the work, wouldn't it be nice to know that the work itself was the reason for the acceptance? After all, you probably intend to try to use it in a book manuscript later and this will help you know if the book is going to make it on its own. But if you are responding to an editor's personal comments on a previous submission by sending more work, address the submission to that editor and thank him for his comments. That should be enough to remind him of what he thought of your previous work.

Multiple simultaneous submissions have become more acceptable over recent years, but as an editor I find them self-defeating to writers in general. It means more material to read for each magazine editor (which already shows signs of slowing down the average response times), it's expensive, and it can be very confusing if you're lucky enough to receive more than one magazine's interest. While there are situations for which it can be necessary, like work that needs to appear in a timely manner because of its subject, I would, as both an editor and a writer, encourage avoiding it.

How long do you wait for a response? At least three months is reasonable, though some magazines will respond faster. If it's getting to be too long, send a short query letter (with a self-addressed stamped envelope included) and wait another month. If you don't hear anything, try somewhere else.

Book publishers are different. Query them first before submitting your manuscript. Check in a general publisher reference work like *Literary Market Place* or *Writer's Market* to be sure your work is suited to their needs and that they will consider work from writers without agents.

Does this seem tedious and slow? It can be. Don't sit around waiting to get famous. Write. Publishing is secondary to the work. It's recognition for a success already achieved. Sometimes you will receive such recognition and sometimes you won't. But if your work is important enough to you, it will carry you through the lean times.

Agents

Some publishers will not read unsolicited work from authors without agents. A good agent will remain aware of who's actively looking for work and who isn't. A good agent will maintain contacts that help your work get looked at. The work must prove itself, but it can't do that if it isn't read. A good agent can save you valuable time that could be spent on your writing instead of on efforts to get published.

But a bad agent is worse than no agent at all. You won't be getting your work out to be seen yourself, believing the agent is doing it. And if the agent isn't, your work isn't getting seen.

Many small presses will read work not submitted through an agent and a publishing record with small presses can open doors to larger presses or become a comfortable home for a writer.

Be aware that it's going to be a struggle for a while. Getting a good agent can be as difficult as getting a publisher.

Start with a reputable list of possibilities. One of the best sources for writers to discover publishing opportunities, including its list of agents, is *Poets and Writers Magazine*. Unlike several of the other writers' magazines available on many newsstands, *Poets and Writers* is a nonprofit organization dedicated to providing helpful information to writers. In other words, they screen their lists. They keep an eye out for bogus and unfair operators. No one can do this completely and you must be careful, but it helps to begin with an information source that is making an effort to eliminate the sleazy and the deceptive.

Scams

An incredible number of people think they may have "inherent" talent as writers. A few might, but they don't get very far without dedication and hard work. Yet the belief persists that one might be "discovered" and made famous for some singular ability received at birth or by some mysterious process of osmosis. And many people believe that just being published somehow entitles you to a valuable air of superiority. This creates opportunity for scam artists.

Among the most common scams are the poetry anthologies. Of course, not all poetry anthologies are scams and opportunities for submitting to the reputable ones can be found listed in places like *Poets and Writers Magazine*. But there are several out there that accept almost anything sent to them. How is this possible? They print thousands of short poems in a thick volume with ten or twelve poems to a page and make back their printing costs plus a very tidy profit from requiring each poet to buy a copy of the volume, usually at a somewhat inflated price over similar volumes on the bookstore shelves, where you will almost never find this kind of book because no serious effort at distribution is made beyond selling to those included. Another poetry scam expects the "finalist" poet to put out several hundred dollars to attend an awards gathering where several valuable prizes will be awarded to some of the lucky finalists. To stay legal, these operations do usually give out the prizes they advertise, but the judges are rarely poets or editors of sufficient reputation to garner any real literary attention at all for the winners and the huge numbers of losers are, in effect, footing the bill for not only the prizes but a substantial profit for the sponsors.

Perhaps the most widely operated scam around is "vanity" publishing. These publishers offer the "services" of a publisher, but are not really publishers. They

144

often have names that sound like publishers. Another term for them is "subsidy" publishers. What this means is that you are expected to pay for the printing and other services. They do not pay you for your work. You pay them to print it. The biggest deception of this type of scam is that a real publisher does a great deal more than print your work. A real publisher does whatever he can to promote it (within his sometimes limited budget) and above all, develops a reputable standing in the book community, which includes the bookstores that might want to put your book on their shelves.

Many university and small presses conduct contests with entry fees from which they publish the winner. This is not the same thing as the above mentioned scams. These contests often have widely known writers as judges and, more importantly, the publishers involved are recognized as serious literary endeavors in the book community and it can enhance any writer's reputation to be published by them. Just remember that the competition is severe. Do not submit to such contests until you are very sure your work is on a par with what's being published in the better literary journals.

"Self-publishing" can be entirely different from vanity publishing but requires that the author become a publisher. Most authors don't know what's really involved in publishing. Volunteer with a non-profit publisher for a while or take a course on publishing first, if you're considering it. Learn what your added job is really going to require of you.

Here are some general guidelines to help steer you away from the scam artists:

1. If you are expected to buy a copy of the magazine or anthology in order to appear in it, it's probably a scam. Watch out for the sneaky ones that claim they don't insist on this but seem to lose your work if you don't buy. Many reputable literary magazines cannot afford

to pay you for your work, but they will send you at least one copy of the issue your work appears in. They may encourage you to purchase additional copies (often at a discounted rate), but they will not require it and they will not lose your work if you don't follow through on purchasing.

2. Check out the publisher and/or judge. If you cannot order the works of either from your local bookstore, it's probably a scam. The most important object of publishing is to get your work seen. If no one besides the other scammed writers included in the work is going to see it, you've wasted your time.

3. Be wary of cash-only contest prizes. If they want to give you money instead of publishing and promoting your work, they're probably getting much more cash back from the operation than they're giving out and that may concern them a great deal more than helping your work to get read. Some reputable cash prizes are awarded, but they are usually not contests open to unpublished manuscripts. These awards are most often for already published literary achievements.

4. Try submitting a very bad piece of work to a magazine, anthology, or publisher that makes you suspicious, under a pseudonym if you wish. If they accept it, you know they're scammers.

5. Pay attention to the acknowledgments page at the front of books of stories and poems. The authors who have achieved enough recognition to make their way into your hands and garner your admiration have most likely gotten there through reputable publications.

6. Many publishers will strongly encourage you to promote your work with readings, appearances, etc. This benefits both the writer and the publisher, but be wary

if it's a requirement of publication (unless you receive a payment for it). Publishers take risks when they decide to publish a work. Sometimes they do so knowing it is likely to result in a financial loss. But if they expect the author to somehow guarantee financial success, their priorities are in the wrong place. Good publishers support themselves financially from the pockets of readers (and sometimes, arts support groups), not writers.

7. Don't lose sight of the more important goal. A writer's career is a life-long struggle to build recognition of his artistic achievement. Money may be a factor in the struggle, but getting your work seen by good editors and other good writers and keeping it available to the public will reap greater rewards over the course of a writer's career, both financially and personally, than opting for a few more dollars for appearing from a publisher with a less consistent literary reputation. A writing career lasts a lifetime and beyond. A few extra bucks disappear quickly.

A Final Word

Writing is work. But it's the kind of work that rewards you for your most serious efforts. Even if no one else sees it.

Your life can be a more enjoyable and enriching place to be when you use writing to help you live it.

Life doesn't need a reason. Neither does writing.

Enjoy.